### ▮▮▮ Praise for DR. DEBRA MANDEL and *YOUR BOSS IS NOT YOUR MOTHER*

"Anyone who finds past wounds getting in the way of present career success will want to read this book. Dr. Mandel realistically describes counterproductive workplace scenarios that result from childhood bruising—and more importantly, tells you how to heal them so that you can reach your full adult potential."

> —Lois P. Frankel, PhD, author of
> *Nice Girls Don't Get the Corner Office*

"*Your Boss is Not Your Mother* covers new territory for women who want to transform their jobs into joys. Dr. Debra Mandel's premise is that emotional bruises can continue to wound in the workplace as old relationship dynamics are acted out again and again with coworkers and bosses. In addition to helpful illustrations of "office drama" that readers will readily recognize, the book is packed with practical advice on how to take inventory of your own behavior and quality-of-work life. Her eight strategies for creating positive work relationships can help every woman discover gainful employment, in terms of job satisfaction as well as salary."

> —Cheryl Dellasega, PhD, author of *Surviving Ophelia,*
> *GirlWars, The Starving Family* and *Mean Girls Grown Up*

"A real eye-opener for women who are stressed out by unhealthy relationships at work. Dr. Debra Mandel shines a clear light on how to identify and break free from re-enacting childhood problems in the workplace. A compassionate and very readable book. I highly recommend it."

> —Susan Forward, PhD, author of *Men Who Hate Women*
> *and the Women Who Love Them, Toxic Parents,* and
> *Emotional Blackmail*

"Dr. Debra Mandel puts us in the driver's seat where we belong. She shows us how to crash through the barriers that come with all bumpy relationships. She teaches us how to empower ourselves by owning our own choices and taking responsibility for our actions. *Your Boss Is Not Your Mother* shows us how to do everything we can to make sure we work well with others—disallowing problem people who make our jobs miserable. This is a truly useful guide to improving workplace relationships."

—Georgia Durante, author of *The Company She Keeps* and president and founder of Performance Two Inc. stunt driving team

"Navigating through office politics is tough. Problem personalities, bad attitudes, and preconceived standards and expectations can make it hard to be at your most productive; everyone needs a little help from time to time. Dr. Debra Mandel provides readers with clear pointers on how to overcome the challenges that each of us face in our work (and even our personal) relationships. Her no-nonsense approach equips readers to be effective communicators. If you're the boss, or if you want to be the boss, you should be reading this book!"

—Paul M. French, CEO Paul French International, Inc.

"Dr. Mandel presents simple, cogent, and thoughtful advice on how to navigate sometimes treacherous work relationships. I highly recommend this to anyone (including men who need a better understanding of these dynamics), but especially those in high-stress work environments."

—Nathan Kahane, producer, *The Grudge* and *Stranger Than Fiction*

# *Your Boss Is*
# *Not Your Mother*

Eight Steps to Eliminating Office Drama
and Creating Positive Relationships at Work

---

**DEBRA MANDEL, PhD**

---

CHICAGO

Printed in Canada.

Library of Congress Cataloging-in-Publication Data
Mandel, Debra.
    Your boss is not your mother : eight steps to eliminating office
drama and creating positive relationships at work / by Debra Mandel.
      p. cm.
    Summary: "A guide to creating and maintaining positive
relationships in the workplace"—Provided by publisher.
    Includes bibliographical references and index.
    ISBN-13: 978-1-932841-16-9 (pbk. : alk. paper)
    ISBN-10: 1-932841-16-4 (pbk. : alk. paper)
    1. Organizational behavior.  2. Transference (Psychology)
3. Emotional maturity.  4. Interpersonal relations.  5. Work—
Psychological aspects.  I. Title.

HD58.7.M37133 2006
658.3'145--dc22

2005017990

In order to protect the anonymity and privacy of my clients, I've changed
their names, circumstances, and other identifying information. In some
cases, I've created composites that closely resemble the experiences of
real people. Any similarity to actual people is coincidental. The information in this book is meant to educate, illustrate, and inspire people
who struggle with drama in their workplace and who want to create a
more positive experience. It is in no way intended to be a replacement
for professional help.

Agate books are available in bulk at discount prices. Single copies are
available prepaid direct from the publisher.

Agatepublishing.com

## DEDICATION

To my mom, who passed away many years ago. Though we weren't able to work out our differences and resulting drama before you left this world, I hope you somehow know that I've always loved you. And because of all of my healing, I can now finally appreciate the gifts I've received from our relationship. These I will always cherish.

# TABLE OF CONTENTS

# INTRODUCTION

For many years I could easily have been the poster girl for vulnerability. I was a raw nerve, unprotected against potential harm. I felt like a full-body bruise that was getting pressed over and over again.

This didn't just happen in my intimate relationships. It affected my entire existence. It wasn't until I reached my early thirties, after a series of disappointing relationships with both intimate partners and professional peers, that I realized my unhealed sore spots from childhood prevented me from feeling safe anywhere. I learned that until I put these behind me I would continue to create havoc and disappointment wherever I went.

After years of anguish and torment, I finally realized that I couldn't take it anymore. I became fed up with letting others take advantage of my "goodness" and tired of thinking that my pain was everyone else's fault. And I hated that other people felt sorry for me. I knew I had resources and talents but I could never really display them as long as I stayed in pity-mode. I knew I needed to find a different path.

Though I could have become depressed by my newfound awareness, I was pleasantly surprised to see that I felt empowered instead. Once I could recognize that I had created my own misery in adulthood, I began walking toward happiness and freedom. I had opened the door to change. And my vulnerabilities became my strengths. Plus, once I was able to simply embrace the fact that it was my job to get better, I noticed profoundly positive changes right away.

I became able to challenge old beliefs and behaviors that led me down dead-end streets, and able to recognize that I was the only enemy keeping me from success. I could then take responsibility for my choices as an adult and fully claim my right to thrive and to live life joyfully. Not only did my personal relationships improve, but so did my professional relationships.

I outlined my methods for healing childhood bruises and creating thriving personal relationships in my first book, *Healing the Sensitive Heart: How to Stop Getting Hurt, Build Your Inner Strength, and Find the Love You Deserve*. Now, I bring you *Your Boss Is Not Your Mother*, your guide to eliminating drama in the workplace and creating positive relationships with your coworkers and boss. After twenty years' experience as a psychologist, I've been fortunate to help hundreds of people mend their tender spots and reach new heights of personal and professional power. I hope that you, too, will reap the same rewards after taking the journey that follows.

In this book, I've primarily focused my examples on women, since my personal and professional experience has taught me that we women are particularly concerned about the quality of our relationships, sometimes even more so than about the job itself. But if you're a guy, please don't turn away. It's great that you too are interested in improving your workplace relationships. In fact, this book can help anyone who wants to have a better workplace experience. So, whatever your gender, status, age, race, or sexual orientation, you can benefit from applying the steps outlined in the chapters to come.

Here are a few of the many people who've encountered workplace woes due to unhealed bruises (as throughout this book, names and other identifying characteristics have been changed):

- Caroline, a thirty-five-year-old account executive, rarely felt satisfied at her job. No matter how hard she worked she couldn't achieve her goals. She lacked motivation and enthusiasm and was always very critical of her own efforts. Oddly, despite her negative self-image, her boss held her in high regard and gave her frequent accolades. But because Caroline wasn't living up to her own rigid standards, she still feared that she would one day be fired.
- Luanne, a forty-eight-year-old engineer, could not get

along with her coworkers. She perceived her peers to be hostile and out to get her and, fearing rejection and disapproval, couldn't trust any of them, even those who went out of their way to befriend her. Yet rather than try to please others by acting nicely, she unknowingly set up situations where she was sure to be disliked. She started arguments by insulting people. She even provoked those who were basically docile. While on a deeper level she desperately craved meaningful social interaction, she couldn't accept this need and instead sabotaged any hope for positive relationships. Why? Because deep down, she didn't believe she deserved respect.

- Katie, a thirty-year-old sales manager, had an unusually high staff turnover even though she went out of her way to create appealing working conditions for her subordinates. She offered flextime, bonuses, and many other positive incentives. She rewarded hard work and gave her staff extra time off when they met sales quotas. Yet despite her efforts to impress them, her employees were dissatisfied. Unknown to Katie, her employees couldn't tolerate her personality. She judged others harshly and often came to work irritable and grumpy. Katie expected her employees to take care of her emotional needs. She would ask them for inappropriate favors, such as to take her clothes to the dry cleaners. Katie often brought her personal relationship problems to the work setting and showed little regard for professional boundaries.

- Sean, a forty-two-year-old teacher, had such deep longings to be admired and approved of by his peers that he constantly went out of his way to do unasked-for favors and tasks in hopes of receiving validation. As though his teaching job weren't demanding enough, he added to his burden by trying desperately to win the affection of his fellow teachers and his pupils. Whenever someone failed to recognize his achievements, he became depressed and felt unworthy.

While on the surface these scenarios differ, they share many similarities. All reflect people who were prisoners of their unhealed bruises continuing to wreak havoc in their professional lives. All of them were unknowingly seeking love, attention, affection, admiration, acknowledgement, and approval from people who couldn't possibly give them whatever they hadn't received in childhood. They were stuck creating and responding to drama, unable to develop the positive relationships they craved and deserved.

Caroline, Luanne, and the others each wanted more gratifying work lives, yet they were trapped in toxic relationship patterns. Each felt victimized and frustrated by others without actually knowing why. They had no idea that they were the creators of their own distress. It wasn't that they disliked their jobs. They simply couldn't enjoy them because they couldn't separate their childhood experiences from their current life situation. They weren't able to recognize their own share of responsibility in the outcome of their interactions—whether negative or positive.

They didn't know that emotional bruises that had originated in their childhoods continued to influence how they related to everyone else. And they had no idea that, if they could only identify these vulnerabilities, and learn how to transform their awareness of them into resources, they could stop wasting precious time trying to get their needs met in the wrong places and by the wrong people. They could instead develop positive workplace relationships and lead happier lives.

At every level of society, millions of women and men suffer from unhealed emotional bruises that get played out in unnecessary drama and conflict in their adult relationships. These old sore spots don't have to be traced to major violations like child abuse, neglect, or abandonment. Nor need they have been intentionally inflicted. Most often, the emotional bruising we suffer developed through relationships with loving caregivers (such as, for example, family members, teachers, babysitters) who unintentionally missed the boat on how to fulfill our developmental needs. Yet these old remnants cause us to misperceive other people's intentions and feel criticized, betrayed, or dismissed by others. We develop expectations of others that simply can't be met. We search for validation in all the wrong places, from all the wrong people. We want our boss or coworker to make up for the things that our mommy, daddy, or sis never provided for us.

Of course, this is not to say that we don't often encounter people in the workplace who abuse power or who act inappropriately. But when we have unhealed stuff in our pasts, we're likely to react to these problem figures more intensely, with childlike behaviors. Conversely, when we get past our emotional hurts, we can see these negative people for who they are and recognize that they would be the last people on earth we'd try to get our needs met from.

Also, while we may expect old unhealed emotional bruises to play a part in our intimate relationships, we're often quite surprised to learn that these same issues can affect our professional relationships as well. We feel that our "professional" workplace attitudes and expectations should insulate us from the kinds of issues that wreak havoc in our less-guarded, more emotionally exposed personal lives. Because we expect ourselves to be better defended against our vulnerabilities at work, we can be taken aback when we discover that our old "stuff" makes no distinction between our personal and professional relationships—all of which can provide fertile ground for negative behavioral and emotional patterns.

While many individuals developed strong coping skills as children to deal with whatever distress they encountered, these same behaviors are often less useful when it comes to handling adult situations. Often they serve only to sabotage those situations. Unfortunately, people struggling with these kinds of problems often become magnets for more pain. Even when they manage to attract competent and emotionally stable people into their lives, they lack the tools necessary to nurture these healthy relationships. In fact, they frequently reject good candidates and flock toward the unhealthy ones.

A person with exposed (or even camouflaged) vulnerabilities in the workplace can run into even more problems than in intimate relationships. With friends, family, and lovers, we're likely to be cut some slack, and we can reasonably expect to be treated more gently. The expectation for such leeway in the workplace, however, is unreasonable because it's not our boss's or coworker's job to fix problems in our lives that they did not create. Their jobs are only to perform the required tasks at hand and to be respectful of others. It's your job to bring professionalism and productivity to work and leave your personal issues outside the office.

Let's face reality. The workplace breeds values that are different than those we cherish when we're not on the clock. For instance, it's normal and healthy in the workplace to want to be the one selected for a promotion above your coworker—whereas it would be much less desirable to use this competitive energy while you're sharing time with friends and loved ones. And it's essential to recognize these differences, especially since most of us spend a huge chunk of our time on the job.

Most workplaces have a hierarchical structure. Hence the environment requires a certain level of competitiveness. And along with competition inevitably comes the potential for failure and rejection. These are hard enough to deal with even if we're able to diminish the effect of childhood leftovers on our attitudes and behavior. Thus, if we're going to make it in the working world, we have to get rid of old baggage to be able to develop the strength and stamina we need to deal with its structure.

Though the relationship element in the workplace may be of utmost importance to many of us, others we encounter may not care about it as much. Some are only concerned with climbing the success ladder, getting promoted, and making more money. They may have little, if any, regard for other people in their path whom they may hurt along the way. While you and I may place a high value on personal fulfillment through positive relationships, we can't expect this to be the goal of everyone around us. So while this book focuses on building positive workplace relationships by letting go of old stuff, it's important to keep in mind that in most people's careers, other considerations coexist alongside with this one.

People play out their old stuff in a multitude of ways in the workplace, but most commonly people do the following:

- sabotage their own success
- expect less than they deserve

- anticipate special, often unreasonable favors from people
- settle for dead-end careers
- won't allow themselves to shine in the presence of others
- need to be "the best" in order to experience self-worth
- desire fulfilling work relationships but can't set them in motion
- get stuck in survival mode, unable to thrive
- allow others to make decisions for them
- focus on work relationships to compensate for the absence of satisfying intimate relationships
- undervalue their own importance
- spend too much time appeasing authority figures
- try to get people who don't really matter in their lives to like them
- feel powerless.

If you see yourself in any of these examples, don't despair. Consider it a signal that it's time to commit to a new approach, a new way to live and work. *Your Boss Is Not Your Mother* will help you shed light on how to spot your old bruises and how to say goodbye to the drama they create. Plus this book can also help remove those blocks that interfere with motivation, advancement, and productivity.

The purpose of this book is to give you tools to do the following:

- become a happier, more fulfilled worker
- become more effective in achieving your own personal goals
- move beyond being a survivor in order to become a thriver
- let go of what you can't control and only take charge of that which is within your own power.

This book is *not* aimed at helping you achieve "success" in the classic sense of making more money, or learning how to get promoted more quickly. It's not about finding the shortest path to the executive suite. However, in my experience, when we learn how to relate better to our workplace peers and create balance between our work life and our personal life, we inevitably increase our chances of traditional success.

So if you want to advance your career, enjoy more fulfillment at work, and free yourself from tumultuous relationships, plunge into the chapters that lie ahead. You will discover how:

- old emotional stuff wreaks havoc in the workplace
- we become emotionally bruised in the first place
- to get rid of negative influences and messages from the past
- to create positive relationships in the professional world
- to thrive even when coworkers or bosses push your sensitivity buttons.

Even if you are one of the fortunate ones who have either resolved your own old hurts or never had any to speak of, this book can also help you. Chances are you work with someone who still carries around a bruise or two, and you'll be better equipped to avoid getting sucked into the negative patterns if you learn tools for spotting them.

This is an interactive book. Hence, I encourage you to set aside time to do more than read it. Take part in its self-tests, exercises, and checklists. Read each anecdote from the perspective of how it might relate to you, and feel free to revisit the sections most meaningful to you.

Also, because we're all unique with our own stories to tell, I may not have addressed your specific situation. If so, then I apologize in advance. Nevertheless, I do hope you'll find an example or two that's close enough so that you can generalize to your own experience.

## A note on terminology

As you'll see throughout the book, I frequently refer to the emotional issues left over from childhood as "bruises." I've used many variations on this word to avoid too much repetition, such as "tender spots," "baggage," "issues," "stuff," and "wounds." But, while I interchange these words, all the while I am referring to emotional sensitivities or vulnerabilities that stemmed from earlier relationships with significant others.

Now let's move onward toward a satisfying, fulfilling work life!

**III** Your Boss Is Not Your Mother

# One

# How Do Bruises from Childhood Create Workplace Chaos?

Millions of women and men go through life carrying around bruises from their past. These result in a vulnerability that leaves them more likely to create chaos, unwittingly, in all of their relationships.

Some people are aware of their bruises and recognize where and how they came about, but they don't yet know how to overcome them. Others feel as if they've been bruised, but still don't recognize the origins of why they're so easily hurt. Still others don't have any idea that they're plagued by this fallout from their childhood experiences, let alone know how to deal with their hurt.

Often people don't recognize they have old injuries because they don't believe they had a right to feel hurt in the first place! Unless they were downright abused or traumatized, people often trivialize their pain, especially if they were hurt unintentionally by a well-meaning caregiver. After all, most of us were told in childhood, "Don't make a mountain out of a molehill." Or we've been told not to dwell on our hurt feelings, which often results in our concluding that those feelings don't really matter.

For instance, Alice's mom got married too young, had kids before she was really mature enough to handle them, and therefore wasn't attentive enough during Alice's formative years. Though Alice's mom loved her, she wasn't able to provide the affection Alice needed to feel fulfilled. But because Alice knew her mother hadn't meant her any harm, and because she wanted to see her mom in a favorable light, she went through her early adulthood believing that she had no right to feel hurt by her mother's neglect.

Despite Alice's attempts to rationalize her mother's behavior, the feelings remained alive and affected her life as an adult, mostly by causing her to seek special favors from people in the workplace. Sometimes Alice would expect coworkers to do more than their fair share of the workload—she'd claim to be "too tired" from all the stresses in her life. Or she would ask her officemates to cover for her by telling their boss that Alice was taking care of important work-related tasks. Usually Alice wouldn't be doing anything related to her job. Rather, she'd more likely be out taking an extra-long lunch break, or repairing the previous night's quarrel with her boyfriend. She had no idea how needy she'd become.

Childhood bruises come from many sources and do not have to be severe to have lasting effects. The people highlighted throughout this book exhibit a whole range of examples of childhood hurts, from severe abuse by family members (physical, sexual, or emotional) to occasional mild slights from teachers, peers, or relatives.

Many of you might be thinking that it doesn't make any sense that your childhood—so far in the past—could possibly have any effect on you in the present, especially if you have never suffered any kind of serious abuse or neglect. That's okay. Just don't rule it out yet. As you'll soon discover, bruises come in all shapes and sizes, from all kinds of sources. And oftentimes they've been so subtle that they've been dismissed from conscious memory. But, if left unhealed, they *will* cause trouble somewhere in your lives, most often in your relationships. While some people manage to keep their sore spots isolated to their most intimate connections, more often, our vulnerabilities bleed into all of our interactions, including into the workplace.

We can't change the fact that whatever we experience has an impact in our lives; nor can we change what has already happened. But we can change how we deal with our old hurts that have never been healed, and we can transform them in ways that work for us rather than against us.

## Where do these bruises come from?

Our emotional bruises can originate in many different ways. The worst, of course, is abusive behavior, such as from neglect or childhood beatings. While abuse may cause the most obvious and most damaging kinds of emotional injury, it's not the only experience that can have a scarring effect. Some emotional bruises can result from events as simple as your dad forgetting your tenth birthday while he was away on a business trip. Or they may have come from chronic emotional disappointments. A wound is a wound, and it can come from anyone or anything.

Also, good intentions don't necessarily erase the resulting bruise. When something hurts, we don't really care *why* it happened. It simply hurts, and it needs proper care and attention in order for it to mend. If someone steps hard on your toe, it doesn't really matter whether it was the outcome of an accident or an intentional act to cause injury. If it's broken, it needs mending. Why it happened may make a difference later, after you've attended to the wound, but until the crisis is fixed, it really doesn't matter.

The same concept holds true for emotional injuries. So often, people are told in their youth that their hurt feelings shouldn't be a big deal. They are told repeatedly not to make a big deal out of nothing. The problem is that the nothing was *something* to them. Therefore, to finally be free of the pain, you need to give yourself full permission to claim and deal with all of your old hurts, no matter how insignificant you may have been told that they were.

Below are some of the ways we become emotionally bruised in childhood. Don't get bogged down by trying to recall all of the ways you may have been hurt. And don't worry if you can't remember all of the details of your own youth. This frequently happens when painful events happened and fix-it opportunities were not provided at the time. Or you may have developed defense mechanisms that keep your memories out of your conscious awareness, to help decrease your suffering. (More on this in Chapter Four.) For now, just keep an open mind to giving your childhood vulnerabilities a context so you can begin getting over them.

There are many influences that affect us when we are young: family (parents, siblings, relatives, stepparents), peers, teachers, friends, religious institutions, hired caregivers (nannies, child-care workers), our social groups, and the media. Generally, our primary caregivers have the most profound influence on our developing identity and self-worth. But the others can also have quite a big impact, especially as we grow beyond our first four or five years.

Usually the bruises that are most intense and long-lasting occur before we reach adolescence. However, emotional injuries can happen throughout our lives. Thus, even if our earlier foundation was pretty strong, a trauma occurring later in childhood can become very debilitating.

Mary's wonderfully loving mother died when Mary was ten. Up until then, she had been lucky to have good parenting, with both her mother and father enriching her life. Unfortunately, after Mary's mom died, her father fell into a deep depression from which he never fully recovered. He hired nannies to take care of Mary and essentially was unable to fulfill her emotional needs. Had her dad withdrawn only temporarily, Mary probably would not have suffered as much. But because his depression lasted so long, and affected his relationship with her so powerfully, it was almost as though her original family foundation was erased.

Sometimes we are fortunate enough to receive some acknowledgement for our bruising at the time the damage occurred. For instance, when a parent acknowledges your pain, apologizes, *and* changes his or her behavior to keep the hurt from recurring, this can provide amazing healing. When Demi's daughter was entering her toddler years, time-outs were the prescribed method of discipline. Demi, of course, wanting to be a good parent, began using time-outs when her little angel became unruly.

As it turned out, while time-outs may have been the method of choice for some kids, it was the worst possible method for Demi's. Fortunately, Demi was strong enough to be less influenced by the need for approval from the outside world, and she was ready to alter her disciplinary tactics even if that meant not doing what was recommended. So, in order to remedy her mistake, she created a time-out zone where she would hold her daughter quietly until the child would calm down.

I am certainly not suggesting that Demi's way is the right way. Time-outs work great for many kids and thus would be the best method of choice for them. But they didn't work for Demi's daughter. Later, when her daughter was about seven, Demi asked her what she remembered being her most distressing moments. Sure enough, the time-outs were at the top of her list. Demi gave her daughter her most sincere apology, and she could see the pain lift from her daughter's face. When she could acknowledge her own mistake, Demi made it safe for her daughter to move on. They are fortunate. Too often, caregivers don't fully understand how to take responsibility for the impact of their behavior on childrens' well-being.

Certainly, it's a good start for a child to have a hurt acknowledged by a parent. But it's not enough. If the caregiver continues to make the same mistake, the bruise will remain alive and unhealed. For example, Patty's dad, Joe, admitted to Patty when she was about nine years old that he was sorry he had a bad temper and yelled at her so often. He promised to correct his behavior. Patty was so grateful for this acknowledgement, but unfortunately, Joe never followed up on his promise. Patty never felt entitled to feel hurt by her dad's behavior—after all, he did *try* to change.

In order for Patty to get past this old bruise, she needed to embrace her right to feel hurt. Not in a way that made her hate her dad. Rather, in a way that would help her see that she was keeping this hurt alive—in her case, by accepting men into her life who mistreated her verbally, such as one of her coworkers.

Now we'll run through the broad categories of how we might get bruised. If I have missed a category that you feel you fall into, please, don't dismiss your experience. Just accept that it's valid, even if I haven't directly addressed it.

## Dysfunction

Dysfunction is ineffectual behavior that can come in the form of words, actions, or beliefs. As a description, it can be applied to the quality of a relationship with others or with ourselves. For instance, if I treat others with kindness and respect, but don't take good care of myself, then I'm demonstrating positive behavior toward others and dysfunctional behavior toward myself. Or if I were to tell my child to do one thing while I'm doing another, I would be role-modeling inconsistent behavior and therefore acting quite dysfunctionally.

I remember my mother forcing me to eat everything on my plate while picking at her own food. Sometimes she would barely eat at all. Later, I understood that she suffered from anorexia nervosa. But in my youth, I was only aware of the inconsistency between what she was *telling* me and what she was *doing*. She thought she was teaching me good eating habits because she wanted me to be healthy and didn't want me to waste food. Unbeknownst to her, she was modeling very inconsistent eating habits. As a result, I wasn't learning to trust my body's cues about hunger and satiation. I also realized that my not wasting food wasn't really doing anything to save the starving children around the world. Ultimately, I ended up having my own significant eating issues as a teenager.

Beth's mother, Pam, thought Beth was an overly sensitive child. She thought she would help Beth deal with adulthood better by encouraging her to develop a thick skin. Whenever Beth showed any signs of hurt feelings, Pam would tell her not to make such a big deal out of nothing. While it's true that Beth would have benefited from not taking everything so much to heart, Pam's approach actually added to the problem. Pam failed to provide the empathy necessary for Beth to be able to develop sound resources to cope when the world seems harsh. As a result, Beth *did* develop a thick skin.

What Pam didn't realize was that a thick skin is no better than a thin skin. Unbeknownst to Pam, she was preventing Beth from learning the option of choosing the skin best fitted to a particular situation. Beneath her tough veneer, Beth remained emotionally vulnerable. Her thick skin only served to alienate her from people who really would be safe for her to get close to. This example highlights how a well-meaning, albeit dysfunctional, intervention can result in even more difficulty!

Dysfunctional behavior is often unintentional and well-meaning. It becomes abusive, however, if it continues in disregard of a child's suffering. If a parent or other influential caregiver in a child's life recognizes that she is causing emotional or physical damage and continues doing so anyway, this enters the realm of abuse. Most of us have issues that stem from dysfunctional behavior.

## Abuse

Abuse comes in many forms: physical, sexual (a specific type of physical abuse), verbal, psychological/emotional. Abuse can be perpetrated by a parent, sibling, relative, friend, teacher, or stranger. It may be persistent or intermittent. A child may not believe the treatment she received was abusive until much later in life, when she recognizes that these behaviors are considered inappropriate by our society, or even illegal.

Many people who abuse children tell the victim that what they are doing is for their own good. When the abuse comes from a trusted caregiver as opposed to a stranger, the child is far more likely to believe the abuser and see herself as deserving the treatment, no matter how hurtful it feels.

In many cases of sexual abuse, the perpetration may not feel bad at all. In fact, children who are sexually violated may experience arousal and pleasure. Many perpetrators are masters at seducing the child into believing that they have invited the molestation and are actually responsible for the perpetrator's actions. But regardless of the child's experience, any sexual act performed on a child is abusive and potentially harmful.

Even if the abuser is a child who would not be held accountable in the same way as an adult, this doesn't make the injury to the victim any less significant. In fact, it's very common for an older child who is being sexually molested or mistreated in some other way to act out by abusing a younger child (maybe a sibling). In this case, both are victims.

Verbal abuse comes in many varieties: name-calling, excessive teasing, telling jokes at a child's expense, yelling, threats of abandonment or physical pain. Warning a child to stop behaving in a way that is inappropriate or dangerous, or else face the consequences, is not abuse.

For instance, if a child keeps smacking his little sister on the head and the parent takes his toys away until he ceases the smacking, the parent is setting a perfectly legitimate consequence. While the child may be annoyed and even feel angry or hurt momentarily, this type of scenario usually wouldn't produce any scarring affects. Plus, children need boundaries for healthy development. When a child understands healthful and appropriate limits, relationships are supported, not destroyed.

However, if the same parent says, "I'm going to put you in your room forever, and I'll never give you anything to eat," that's carrying the consequence too far. This could certainly cause bruising in the long run and clearly borders on abuse, even if the threat is never carried out.

All of the above (physical, sexual, and verbal abuse) qualify as psychological/emotional abuse as well. But the category of psychological/emotional abuse also encompasses all those things that are less easily defined, but still potentially damaging to a child's development and well-being.

For instance, a parent who teaches a child not to cry (as the parent believes this is a sign of weakness despite evidence to the contrary) is actually being emotionally abusive. A child's fundamental need and right to be able to express emotions in the body's natural form is being restricted. This cannot lead to any good outcome. Helping a child learn how to modulate emotions and find outlets for expression would be healthy, but censoring the existence of emotions altogether is very harmful. Anything that repeatedly and intentionally shames, degrades, or devalues a child's interests, needs, and opinions constitutes psychological/emotional mistreatment.

Paula's brother constantly poked fun at Paula's developing body. Though her parents could see how much this was affecting her body image and sense of self-worth, they never intervened. On occasion, her dad would tell him to stop—but Dad never followed through with any consequences. In fact, sometimes Paula's mom, whom Paula thought would at least be on her side, would start picking on Paula as well. Her mom would even call her "chubby" in a disapproving way.

Paula spent so much time in adulthood worrying about the shape of her body (which was perfectly healthy) that she had trouble getting her work done. She feared that others thought that she was fat and ugly. She was constantly counting calories and checking herself out in the mirror. She could have finished fifteen extra marketing reports each week in the time she spent ruminating about her appearance. The irony was that her coworker (who was thirty pounds heavier than Paula) got a promotion they had both desired.

## Neglect and Abandonment

Neglect can be just as devastating to our well-being as acts of maltreatment. The deprivation of love, touch, nurturing, and/or care leaves a child frightened and helpless. While many abused kids grow up wishing that they had just been left alone, those who were neglected fantasize about having had contact—any contact, even abuse seems better than nothing. (Of course, in reality neither is desirable).

As adults we often consider "alone time" as a gift. Time to ourselves, without outside pressure, allows us the necessary space to gather our thoughts, replenish our energy, and reconnect with our inner selves. This is also necessary for healthy development in our youth.

But when this is the norm of a child's existence, especially a young child, it can be harmful to development. It's through the loving involvement of a caregiver that a child develops a positive self-image. If this isn't provided, the child has nothing to hold onto. Young children require an adult to be a present, available, ongoing source of nurturance to be able to build trust and develop the capacity to become an independent, functioning, and thriving adult. They simply cannot tolerate long periods of aloneness without suffering severe consequences. Neglect or threats of abandonment keep a child in a chronic state of survival mode—in terror of death.

The above examples depict the most severe kinds of neglect or abandonment. There are many more subtle varieties. Some of these are:

- Caregivers who are always preoccupied and emotionally unavailable.
- Caregivers who suffer some form of mental disorder (e.g., depression, anxiety, posttraumatic stress disorder) that interferes with their capacity to meet a child's needs.
- Caregivers who become physically compromised and then fail to provide a substitute parental figure. For instance, if Mom or Dad becomes injured and immobile, a child may become permanently housebound if called upon to care for the disabled parent.
- Caregivers who haven't healed their own childhood bruises or have not become aware of them. They may unconsciously or consciously use the child as a surrogate parent.
- Caregivers who use a child consciously or unconsciously as a stand-in spouse.
- Caregivers who place a child in a position where she is expected to handle tasks and chores she is not developmentally ready for. I know of one woman who was actually making her own breakfast at age two because her mother wanted to sleep late.
- Caregivers who leave children with someone ill-equipped to adequately care for them (e.g., having a seven-year-old babysit for a three-year-old).

Many times these kinds of circumstances arise from unforeseen situations. For example, Jack's parents divorced when he was about five. Up until then, his parents made a pretty good living. However, shortly after the divorce, his dad lost his high-paying job and, too proud to take a lesser one, remained unemployed for two years.

He was stressed out most of that time and consumed with feeling like a failure.

During that time, Jack's mom was working up to sixty hours a week and coming home from work exhausted. Jack spent long hours in after-school day care. This could have been fine had either his mom or dad spent any quality time with him at all. But Jack actually received more attention at day care than at home.

Understandably, Jack's mom was trying to make ends meet. However, she was no more available during her nonworking hours because she was both too tired and too absorbed with her resentment toward Jack's father. Hence Jack received only minimal care.

Jack's parents could have made different choices that might have served Jack's development better. But Jack truly loved his mom and dad. They were never mean to him, they always told him they loved him, and, on the rare occasion that he had the full attention of either of them, he was in heaven. Nevertheless, he had an ever-present aching feeling of sadness and emptiness. He learned to adapt to his childhood loneliness by becoming highly skilled at entertaining himself using his creative imagination. However, as an adult, he isolated himself from others. He had very few relationships, convincing himself that he didn't need anyone in his life. At his workplace, he had poor social skills and wasn't a natural team player. One day, this shortcoming cost him a promotion for which he had worked very hard.

## Societal Insults and the Media

Our families, relatives, teachers, and peers have the biggest influence on our development—their impact ranks right up there with our genetics and temperament. But, since the people who are responsible for our care as children are part of a larger culture, we cannot escape the influence of societal norms and beliefs, and how we see people and situations portrayed in the media. And there remains a great deal of prejudice, racism, gender stereotyping, homophobia, sexism, and a general intolerance for differences between people. These factors can cause and inflame emotional bruises.

People who have been spared feeling exploited or oppressed may have a hard time appreciating how painful this can be for others who have been on the receiving end of oppression. Lisa, whose family came to America from Korea when she was two, grew up in a predominantly white middle-class neighborhood. Hers was the only Asian family in the area, but during her earliest years, she barely noticed that she was viewed differently. By the time she started school, however, everything had changed. There she was harassed and called horrible names because of her race. Her parents did not know how to handle the situation. They tried to console her when she would come home crying, but that didn't put a stop to the constant insults she endured.

Jim knew he was different from his friends before he even knew the words "homosexual" or "gay." But it didn't seem to matter until he was in high school and all of his friends started dating. He was terrified of the ridicule he would face if he were to come out and express his preference to date guys, and he suffered tremendous shame for his sexual orientation. As a result, these feelings forced him into a life of denial and secrecy. He wanted so much to be liked by his peers that he faked an interest in girls. He felt he had to live a lie in order to avoid being rejected.

Both Lisa's and Jim's experiences dealt huge bruises to their sense of self-worth. This affected every aspect of their lives. In the workplace, both lacked confidence and feared ridicule and disapproval from coworkers. They had tremendous difficulty being honest with themselves and others.

## Turning It Around

Most children who have suffered childhood mistreatment do not grow up to abuse others. In fact, they grow up to continually mistreat themselves. Mistreated children often grow into adulthood suffering problems with self-esteem, feelings of guilt or shame, unresolved anger, and irrational fears and insecurities. Their relationships are often tumultuous and filled with angst and pain. Their work relationships are often characterized by unnecessary conflict and drama.

Even those who think they weren't affected by their leftover vulnerabilities almost always carry some lasting effects that interfere with their ability to thrive. Adults who recognize that they are affected by childhood bruises, but who haven't yet figured out how to heal them, frequently show similar signs of self-destructive behavior and similar problems with self-care.

Human beings are complicated creatures with many complex needs. In a perfect world, all of our caregivers and all of the important people in our lives would support and encourage all of our needs. But no one lives in this perfect world. Most of us haven't had all of the love and nurturing that we need and want. So it's natural that we grow into our adulthood with some unfilled holes.

As we seek out other people in the world to help fill in these holes, we too often end up disappointed and hurt once again. It usually fails to occur to us that other people too are walking around with their own bruises and other old stuff. When our old stuff encounters other people's, no one really has anything positive to throw into the mix.

Some people wish that they could have been spared many of the experiences they had as children. I know many who believe that they would have picked a different family if they were given the option. They even believe that, if given the chance, they would have picked an entirely different life.

I hope to show you that there's no need to ever again wish you'd had a different life. Believe it or not, difficult and painful experiences you've endured and suffered can become your treasures you cherish. You have not been damaged—affected, yes, but not ruined. And once you learn how to transform these wounds into resources, you will embrace them—and your relationships will improve tremendously.

The source of feeling better is right at our fingertips—within our own selves! Once we discover this beautiful and empowering reality, we unlock the door to our prison of pain and can set ourselves free.

If any of the above descriptions resonate with you, you're probably affected by "old stuff." The question is, "How and to what degree does this affect you in the workplace?"

Go ahead and find out. I encourage you to take the following test. Even if you don't think you resemble any of the descriptions I outlined above, take the test anyway. You've really got nothing to lose. Sometimes the presence of old stuff affecting your life is not obvious at first. Or you might want to take the test on behalf of someone you think may be stuck in her past.

I can almost guarantee that at some point in your life you'll encounter someone whose childhood leftovers are dominating the interaction. Thus, the more you understand, the better equipped you will be to have positive relationships with others.

## The Test:
## How Does Your "Old Stuff" Affect You in the Workplace?

If you are consciously aware of your "old stuff," you probably won't be shocked by your responses to many or most of these questions. And if you're reluctant to admit that you have any leftover vulnerabilities because you consider it a sign of weakness, then let me remind you of something very important: the best way to deal with your painful or adverse experiences isn't to deny them, but to transform them into resources.

Keep in mind that the presence of old wounds shows no favoritism to race, gender, intelligence, socioeconomic status, or profession. You could be a lawyer, doctor, engineer, secretary, caterer, contractor, salesperson, postal worker, or electrician. I could go on and on—name a profession, and I'll show you many wounded birds among them.

Let's also debunk the myth that people with wounds cannot be successful. Quite the contrary. In fact, you yourself have probably already managed to achieve a measure of success in life. But regardless of where you stand on the success ladder, you can benefit from looking deeper into the subtle ways your old stuff may be keeping you from shining even more. Or if you're truly free of leftover stuff, read on anyway. If nothing else, you can learn how to keep from getting sucked into the chaos of someone else's issues running amok. And you can develop greater compassion and empathy for others—two very important qualities for creating positive workplace relationships (or any other kinds of relationships).

Most importantly, I encourage you to keep an open mind. Our vulnerabilities become our strengths only once we acknowledge and embrace them. Thus, the more you grasp the reality of where you might be stuck, the quicker you'll progress.

Now: read the following twenty questions, and choose the response that best describes how you feel most of the time. Then add up your total score. There are no trick questions here. And keep in mind that you don't have to share your responses with anyone but yourself, so be very candid. After all, if you aren't honest because you're too embarrassed to admit the truth, it will only delay your progress.

*Scoring key*
Never (0 points)          Frequently (3 points)
Seldom (1 point)          Always (4 points)
Sometimes (2 points)
*Give yourself a 0, 1, 2, 3, or 4 according to your answer to each question.*

1. Do you feel disrespected by your coworkers, bosses, and/or employees?
2. Do you expect coworkers, bosses, or employees to be your friends?
3. Do you expect or wish that coworkers, bosses, or employees would grant you special favors when you perform below standard, such as when you've been out sick, shown up late, or missed a deadline?
4. Do you wish that your boss or coworkers appreciated you more?
5. Do you take responsibility for the workload of others who are slacking off?
6. Do you have a fear of conflict that keeps you from speaking up about unfairness?
7. Do you censor yourself because you fear being fired or hurting someone's feelings?

8. Do you go out of your way to befriend people in the workplace whom you would not want to be friends with outside of the workplace?
9. Do you envy other people's success?
10. Do you have trouble keeping boundaries with your coworkers (e.g., you let them know things about your personal life that have nothing to do with your work situation)?
11. Do you feel hurt or become defensive when you receive criticism about your work performance?
12. Do you ever feel that others in your field judge you harshly even when no one has voiced criticism?
13. Do you have difficulty not thinking about your work or the workplace when you are supposed to be enjoying free time?
14. Do you have difficulty evaluating your own job performance?
15. Do you become argumentative with coworkers, bosses, or employees?
16. Do you believe you are not living up to your full potential?
17. Do you keep yourself from excelling in the presence of others for fear of their envy or jealousy?
18. Do you let others make decisions for you, even when your gut tells you it's the wrong choice for you?
19. Do you have difficulty saying "no" to unreasonable requests from coworkers, bosses, or employees?
20. Do you withhold your honest opinions about work-related issues for fear that you'll be disliked?

_____ YOUR TOTAL SCORE

Once you've finished and added up your score, refer to the evaluation below to discover how much your old baggage continues to affect you in your workplace. Don't judge yourself harshly if you score high. There's nothing wrong with you! If you are just now discovering that you have some emotional bruises, you couldn't possibly have known that they could interfere with your work. And, even if you have known about them, you've never been given the code for connecting the dots.

If you score between 0 and 5, you most likely only have minimal traces of emotional bruising. You probably do not suffer too much in the workplace. However, since this is not rocket science, it's also possible that the test may not be picking up on some of the subtleties of your vulnerabilities.

Even if you don't personally relate, you might become better able to spot someone in your workplace (or in your personal sphere) who does. If this is the case, you can be helpful in keeping the interactions on a positive note by understanding the dynamics operating in others.

Level One:    6–25
Level Two:    26–55
Level Three:  56–80

Level One: You suffer only a small amount of emotional sensitivity that carries over in the workplace. You may have done some emotional repair work already, or your childhood bruises were not the type or the intensity that would lead to too much difficulty in your adult life. Or they may only surface in intimate relationships, where you are most vulnerable. That's great, but it doesn't necessarily mean you are living up to your full potential. You could still profit from learning some new tools to help you thrive.

Level Two: You probably have a significant amount of distress in your day-to-day life that inevitably bleeds into the workplace. While you're probably pretty good at setting healthy limits with many people in the workplace, a few workmates may push your buttons, and you're likely to struggle with them. You may even be aware while this is happening, or at least shortly after, but you can't seem to stop the reflex. You're probably puzzled when this happens and torment yourself trying to understand "why?" You don't experience yourself as having many, if any, unhealed bruises, but you're constantly struggling to keep things balanced. You don't often feel peace of mind. You most likely experience pressure to perform to unrealistic standards, and unknowingly expect others to make up for something you didn't get from childhood.

Level Three: You probably experience distress a great deal of time. You're using up much more energy managing emotional sensitivities than you are in performing your duties. You may be exhausted from trying to please people, especially those who will likely *never* be pleased. You're easily hurt by others and don't feel very good about yourself. You may have used the workplace as a substitute for truly intimate relationships in your personal life. Or you may be relying on inappropriate people or sources in the workplace to solve your problems from your personal life. You may feel like a slave to your job—trapped with nowhere to go. You probably take responsibility for things you can't really control and therefore have no energy or motivation to take charge of the things that you actually can control. You may have times where you feel like a young child with no options other than to become enraged, frustrated, or helpless. You desperately want to feel better, but because you keep going to empty wells for water, you're parched most of the time. But don't worry—there is a way out!

As painful as it can sometimes be to acknowledge that we have problems, it is the process of admitting to our issues that allows us to pave the way toward growth and empowerment. So, read on, get rid of the chains of the past, and finally take joy in one of the biggest parts of your life—YOUR WORK!

# Two

# Darcy's Story: Old Stuff in Action

To better understand the havoc unhealed bruises cause in the workplace, let's meet Darcy. Her story will help you see how vulnerabilities can lead to workplace drama, the costs to career and workplace relationships, and the benefits of getting rid of old stuff once and for all. Then, we'll also revisit the people described in the Introduction, so you can see their positive transformations as well. I hope this chapter will give you optimism and inspiration.

## Darcy's Story

Darcy, a vivacious and extremely creative thirty-year-old woman, was ready to quit her job and change her career by the time she had arranged to come see me. She couldn't take dealing with her boss anymore—the long hours he demanded (with no appreciation, let alone extra pay or comp time), the insults, the sarcasm, and the degrading comments he routinely made about women. She worked hard, took her job seriously, and forever tried to please this impossible boss. Though she loved her work as an artist and designer, she felt demeaned every day she set foot into her office.

Darcy had worked in advertising for a couple of firms before she got her job at this company. While she had experienced her share of problems at her previous workplaces, this situation was by far the worst. Yet no matter how much her boss mistreated her and no matter how much she wanted to leave, for some reason Darcy felt obliged to stay.

She made excuses for her boss. At times, she even blamed herself for not working hard enough. She actually believed she might be responsible for his ill-tempered behavior. It was as though she were a fly caught in a spider web with no escape.

As Darcy's struggle in her workplace continued, her marriage became increasingly strained. As you can imagine, she had only so much energy left for an intimate relationship. While she and her husband had usually been good at enjoying their free time together, Darcy became increasingly preoccupied. She was less available as a loving partner. She began losing sleep, stopped eating well, and spent hours trying to figure out ways to please her boss, all to no avail.

It especially disturbed Darcy that she would be in this mess since she'd already seen a therapist for intimacy/relationship problems a few years back. She thought for sure that she had completed working on her issues and couldn't believe that she could have so much turmoil in her life, especially at her workplace. After all, her relationship with her boss wasn't intimate at all. She didn't even consider him to be a friend. He was just a boss. Yet for reasons she had yet to figure out, he had enormous power over her feelings of self-worth.

"Why?" I asked her, since Darcy agreed that anyone else in her position would tell this man to take a hike.

Darcy had no idea that she was transferring unresolved, unhealed pain from her childhood into her workplace with her boss. Until she could connect the dots to her childhood pain, she had no way of interrupting this negative process she had created. In fact, as we'll see in a moment, she had unknowingly turned her boss into the image of her father and herself into a helpless child, thus re-creating the dysfunction she experienced with her real father.

As a child, Darcy could never please her father. Though he was a successful and well-respected man in their community, at home he was irrational, harsh, sometimes even cruel. He had a general disregard for other people's needs and felt entitled to more than his fair share in life. Darcy spent the bulk of her youth suppressing her own dreams and trying to please her father. She was expected to cater to his whims and desires.

As a typical example, one night when she was about ten years old, Darcy came to her dad for comfort. That day her best friend had told her that she no longer wanted to be friends. (We all know how cruel other kids can sometimes be.) Darcy explained to her dad that she had told her friend about a rumor that others were spreading about her, but that she needn't worry. Darcy further explained that she had told her friend that she would stand by her no matter what. But Darcy's friend thought that Darcy was the one spreading the rumor, and shunned her. Darcy was devastated.

Because Darcy saw her father as a pillar of strength, she went to him, hoping for helpful words of wisdom. But he didn't offer wisdom at all. Instead, he said, "Go sulk somewhere else, I'm watching TV." Ouch for Darcy. As though the loss of her friend hadn't caused enough pain, once again her efforts to seek comfort and approval from her dad had failed.

Though she had two other siblings, they were less affected by their father's demeanor. Plus, he seemed to expect less of them. In fact, they were jealous of Darcy because she at least got more attention—albeit negative—while their dad pretty much ignored them.

Darcy, the overachiever of the bunch, hated it when she disappointed her father and made it her mission to prove that she was worthy of his admiration and love. What Darcy had failed to grasp was that her father could never really be pleased because he wouldn't take responsibility for his own misery. No matter how many cartwheels she performed, he just wasn't able to appreciate her.

Darcy had no idea that as an adult she brought this pain and disappointment to the workplace. How? She often spent unnecessary time trying to get people to see her in a positive light, even if those people were too messed up themselves to ever see her clearly. She wanted her boss—a man much like her father, stuck in similar misery—to recognize and value her. What she didn't realize was that as long as her boss blamed the world for his unhappiness, he would never be able to take responsibility for how his behavior affected others. And every minute she spent hoping that he would change was time she was taking away from her own growth and professional advancement.

Because Darcy had never had another boss who had pushed these old buttons, the issue had lain dormant until she started working for her present boss. When her father had died during her early twenties (Darcy was thirty-two when she came to see me), she was certain that these issues had gone to the grave with him. But in fact, her father's hurtful behavior continued to have an impact long after his death.

Darcy's journey required her to recognize these old bruises, acknowledge their presence in her adult life, and take responsibility for her own betterment. She needed to stop focusing on what her boss was doing to hurt her. Instead, she needed to magnify what *she* was bringing to the situation that continued to cause her pain: what actions *she* was or wasn't taking, how *she* was sabotaging her own work satisfaction, and how *she* kept herself a victim.

Through our work together she became aware that she was trapping herself by responding to her boss as though she were still a child dependent on her unkind father. And by learning about her childhood hurts and how they could bubble up in her workplace relationships, she realized that she would need to develop a new perspective on herself in order to thrive in the workplace. She had to become fully conscious that this other man, her boss, was *not* her father—and she had to relate to him in a new way.

Darcy had to learn how to take care of business without needing so much acknowledgment from her boss, including how to express her opinions and expectations in a healthy way. She had to stop turning herself into a child, one who feared punishment or disapproval, and start turning her old emotional bruises into qualities like compassion, empathy, and kindness of spirit—that is, into assets that would work for her rather than against her in the workplace.

Through the process outlined in this book, Darcy started to respect herself and claim her right to respectful treatment from others. She made peace with the fact that by asserting herself with confidence, she ran the risk of being fired. But this reality became much easier for her to swallow once she realized that getting fired (which formerly had been her worst fear) wouldn't actually be the end of the world and wasn't in her control anyway. Ultimately, she came to understand that her constant efforts to appease her boss never really eliminated the risk of being fired anyway.

At first, Darcy tried to work things out with her boss by setting limits. She told him that she would no longer be willing to work overtime unless she would be compensated financially or with extra time off. She learned how to speak up for herself when he shouted at her and bullied her. She developed some key phrases like, "I would love to hear your input, but I don't listen very well when you raise your voice." And "I'll be happy to do the extra work. How will I be compensated?"

Being more assertive was scary to Darcy at first. But once she no longer lived by the need to please her boss, she learned that she felt much freer to express herself.

Much to Darcy's surprise, her boss actually became a little less unpleasant. He didn't fire her. However, she ultimately decided that both she and her work would flourish more in a different, more supportive environment. She set out to find another job, armed with a new attentiveness to how prospective employers treated their employees. When she found a good match, she gave her resignation and moved on. Three cheers for Darcy!

Her decision to leave wasn't what signified her success. Others may have chosen to stay. Rather, the key was that she now felt like she had the *option* to leave and the ability to choose according to her own needs. For Darcy, it served her better to make the break. And she could claim full responsibility for asserting this choice.

Darcy's life improved considerably. She became happier and lighter-hearted. Of course, her husband was thrilled. He now lived with a loving companion again, instead of an emotionally distant, irritable grump. Once Darcy came to understand that she was re-creating her old stuff in the present, she could then recognize where and how this process was happening, not only with work relationships but also with all of her other relationships. This awareness gave her the power to change her life and finally begin to thrive.

Darcy's story highlights some of the characteristics of people who have unhealed bruises. Though they all differ in their specific symptoms and they each have their own unique story, these people share many similarities that play out in the work environment. When we carry around old stuff, we commonly:

- take responsibility for things we have no control over.
- have trouble taking responsibility for things we *do* have full control over—like our own behavior, thoughts, and feelings.
- have trouble declining others' unrealistic demands.
- add to our burden by setting unrealistic goals for ourselves.
- live in fear of people's negative reactions, and often doubt our own perception of reality.
- unknowingly set up and/or engage in dead-end power struggles.
- allow ourselves to interact with people who treat us badly, and stay far too long in situations where we feel trapped and disrespected.
- impulsively leave situations where we could possibly benefit from conflict resolution, because we may lack the necessary skills to distinguish hopeless situations from positive, challenging ones.
- repeat negative patterns of relating to others because we re-encounter, in our heads, all of the negative messages we learned in childhood from important caregivers, other influential people, the media, or the culture at large.

I've treated hundreds of women and men in a variety of work settings, most of whom have enormous potential for advancement in their jobs and careers. Yet despite their best efforts, and their endless attempts to incorporate all of the sound business advice floating around, they remain stuck. They can't seem to get it together, and they feel unfulfilled no matter how hard they try.

In my twenty years of clinical experience, I've concluded that to be more effective in the workplace, we need something more and different than traditional motivational or inspirational tools, and far more than advice on how to improve communication. We need a whole new way of understanding our problems, and a whole new repertoire of behaviors. Each of us needs to learn how to heal any unresolved childhood bruises and learn to live in present reality.

When we carry our old bruises into the workplace, we usually do so with little awareness of the *choices* we have about how we relate to others. We lack real knowledge of what it means to behave professionally. We don't know when or how to leave destructive situations. We are not even able to embrace the abundance of self-help and other resources that offer us tools on how to get ahead, increase our motivation, and enhance our productivity. But with the right direction, we can embrace all of the opportunities and resources available to us. We can finally be free to accomplish the goals we desire.

Remember Caroline, the account executive who couldn't live up to her own perfectionistic standards? She discovered that she was reliving old stuff she eventually traced back to growing up with her chronically unhappy mother. Caroline was never given permission to relax and enjoy free time. Though Caroline was a straight-A student who did all her chores without being asked, her mother called her lazy whenever Caroline wanted to just chill out.

Because Caroline had never grasped the deep effect her mother's treatment had on her, she didn't realize that she had begun acting just as her mother had. She continually raised the bar, never able to achieve satisfaction. She thought it was everyone else who put the pressure on her, but she actually created it herself. When she finally realized this, she started to ease up on herself. Needless to say, her work life became much more enjoyable.

Luanne, the engineer, and Katie, the sales manager, realized that they were expecting far too much emotionally from their co-workers. They had to learn to develop social lives outside of the workplace and get their needs met from loved ones instead of from colleagues.

Sean, the schoolteacher, discovered that one of his bruises traced back to having been compared unfavorably to his older brother.

Though Sean was a loving and generous child, well liked by all, he was treated as second best to his successful brother, who was always referred to as "the brainy one." This haunted him wherever he went. Sean had no idea that he kept this old sensitivity alive by always internally comparing himself to his brother. He never acknowledged his own gifts and always believed he fell short. Hence, he constantly needed others to validate his worthiness. Eventually he learned how to appreciate his own individuality and uniqueness and dole out regular doses of self-affirmations.

## Beating Blame

If you're reading this and you think that my approach is harsh and insensitive, I completely empathize. It may even sound as if I'm blaming you for the things you had no control over. But I think as you read on, you'll see that the reason why I focus so much on how important it is to accept responsibility for your own life, now that you're an adult, is so that you can ultimately learn what it means to feel a sense of your own power. In fact, from here on, I encourage you to simply toss out the word "blame" from your vocabulary and instead replace it with either "accountability" or "responsibility."

The first time I realized that my problems in my adult life were of my own creation and that other people would never be able to fulfill the role of caregiver (I had to do that for myself), I felt devastated all over again. "You mean that I have to take responsibility for my own life, and no one else can do that for me?" I questioned despairingly. "This is such a lonely existence."

But as lonely and painful as my learning curve has sometimes been, these insights have worked. Plus, I no longer feel alone after all! I've embraced my own resources and have grown to see myself as a treasure chest filled with precious gifts. You can, too.

In the chapters that follow, I give you what I believe to be the eight essential ingredients for eliminating workplace drama and creating positive relationships. You may already have some of these working for you, so you may decide to skip the chapters that reflect the strengths you already possess. Or you may decide that you might benefit from a refresher course in these areas, and choose to go ahead and read them anyway. Though each chapter is written to build on the last, you may want to skip around to those that are most appealing. You can always go back and read them in sequence. Nevertheless, however you dive into the process, do so with curiosity and empathy in order to get the most out of the tools and examples presented in this book.

# Three

# Eight Steps to Saying Goodbye to Workplace Drama and Hello to Positive Relationships

Believe it or not, the bruises created by your previous experiences can't permanently damage you, and neither can the dysfunctional ways you may have learned to cope with your hurts, no matter how bad they were. Yes, you have been affected—maybe even halted in your tracks—but not ruined. With new tools you learn here, you can become a magnet for positive relationships that will support your professional success. And when office drama threatens to enmesh you, you'll be able to escape its snares. This defines the process of becoming a *thriver*—not just a survivor of the day to day, but someone who flourishes, no matter the situation.

I know this because it happened to me. Believe me. I haven't always had such a positive attitude toward adversity. There was a time in my life when I envied just about everyone else, when I thought other people were always better off than I was, when I saw myself as a victim of life's circumstances. What was even more tragic was that I was so trapped in the "glass-half-empty" mentality that I wasn't able to appreciate all the wonderful gifts I had received in my youth, which included experiences in many foreign countries, a strong work ethic, a sense of perseverance, and a great education. I actually had a great deal to be grateful for. My parents had given me far more tools than I could appreciate at the time. Yet I couldn't see past my own despair.

I had no idea that I was keeping myself mired in place. I believed that I was permanently impaired by my childhood bruises and traumas. The best I thought I could do in life was just to survive. I believed that thriving was reserved for those who were lucky enough to get all of life's goodies, especially lots of unconditional love, acceptance, and praise.

It took me years to see the light beyond the darkness in which I was stuck. Though I had great therapists who were telling me that I deserved all of the good stuff I hadn't yet received in life, none of them was actually showing me how to change the destructive thought patterns and behaviors that (it turned out) I was vehemently holding onto. No one was showing me how I could learn to supply these goodies for myself, and how to kick into gear all the positive resources that I already had right at my disposal.

I was lucky. Through my own trial and error, I developed a process that helped me end my misery. I can no longer imagine ever wishing to have anyone else's life but my own. This process is what I've written here in order to pass along to you.

Once I learned to accept that the difficulties I had endured made me stronger, not weaker, I became able to relate to others in much better, more positive ways. And I was finally able to stop turning other people I encountered in the workplace into substitute caregivers, who would inevitably disappoint me. I also became better at disengaging myself from other people's struggles, so that I could have compassion and empathy for them without having to personalize their problems in ways that caused me more pain.

Of course, many people who got less than they deserved of love, acceptance, and positive regard in their early lives don't necessarily wear their pain on their sleeve the way I had when I was younger. You might be among the many who have developed defense mechanisms, emotional armor that shielded you from feeling pain, even to the extent of your being unaware of your remaining bruises. These defenses come in many forms, from denial to rationalization to outright manipulation. Some people even resort to lying, to others and to themselves, in order to avoid emotional pain. Nevertheless, despite how well these defenses can protect you in terms of keeping you unaware of your hurts, they won't actually solve the effects of your unhealed bruises. Your behavior in the workplace will still be less than ideally functional. If you use defenses like these, you'll need to learn how to let go of them and willingly expose yourself to the vulnerability that lies beneath them. (If you're unaware that you have any such defenses in place, I'm pretty sure you'll figure this out as we go along. And you should pay particular attention to the information in Chapter Four.)

However you cope with your unhealed bruises, you won't be able to transform them, and begin building positive workplace relationships, until you can do the following:

- Acknowledge your own unique vulnerabilities
- Examine how your old stuff plays out in your professional life
- Let go of unrealistic expectations regarding workplace relationships
- Create workplace conditions that support rather than stifle your professional and personal advancement
- Disengage from power struggles
- Learn when to stay and when to quit
- Become more lighthearted and playful while simultaneously maintaining professionalism.

To make this transformation, you must make a commitment to stick it out through this process. It requires patience and dedication—qualities that are sometimes in short supply for the emotionally vulnerable, but which are very important to being able to thrive in the workplace. However, before we can move forward to the eight steps, you must first understand the obstacles that could get in the way of your success.

The roadblocks to taking charge of your life at work include anything you do that impedes your ability to move in the direction you desire. Though there are all kinds of ways we can sabotage our journeys, I've highlighted what I've seen as the two most common roadblocks among people with old bruises: shame and procrastination.

## Shame

Shame is the biggest potential roadblock to making any positive change. Of course, not all shame is negative or debilitating. Shame in small doses helps keep people civil and morally sound. It helps us recognize when we are behaving in ways that are hurtful to others. However, for many people, the levels of shame they experience far exceed its value. And because so many people with old stuff believe that the emotional bruises they suffered in childhood were their own fault, they have become masters at shaming themselves. Their shame levels have often become toxic. In fact, their shame begets more shame, which in turn begets more shame, in an increasing spiral. Once this "shame spiral" ensues, it feeds off itself and becomes ever more resistant to change.

To combat this destructive cycle, you must pay close attention to any moments or situations where you find yourself feeling embarrassed or ashamed. You may discover things about yourself of which you are not very proud. But as you grow to understand that all of your behaviors and ways of coping, however you feel about them now, evolved because at one time they served a very valuable function, you'll be able to stop seeing them in an ill light.

In fact, it's *because* of the bruising that you've suffered that you are better equipped to deal with the dysfunctions that are prevalent in every work environment. You simply need to learn how to let these experiences inform the way you look at your life now in order to keep from getting sucked into the chaos.

The purpose of taking the magnifying glass to your behavior is not to find the flaws. Instead it's simply to find out what is there, both good and bad. When the shame and its sources are identified, you can then make rational choices about what to keep and what to throw away.

Patricia was a master when it came to attacking herself. She would constantly apologize for her existence and frequently called herself "stupid." Both of her parents had been very dismissive and degrading of her intelligence. Unbeknownst to Patricia, her parents were actually threatened by how bright she was. Hence, Patricia was never able to truly appreciate her smarts.

Despite her negative demeanor, she had climbed the ranks at her job and was in charge of about ten employees. But because Patricia was so burdened by shame, she wasn't able to enjoy her managerial role. Her employees liked her, but they didn't treat her respectfully because it was obvious to them that she didn't respect herself.

Patricia's subordinates often questioned her judgment, and they continually pushed back on her by asking for extra time off and special favors. Because Patricia displayed so much self-doubt and self-degradation, she made it easy for her subordinates to take advantage of her. She had tremendous difficulty saying "no" to others' unreasonable requests. While she would usually end up pushing forward with the decisions that she believed were best for the company's success, she found the process to be painstaking and quite unfulfilling.

Patricia realized that she constantly put herself down to in order to avoid the shame she'd felt as a child for being ridiculed. She *expected* that others would mistreat her the way her parents had. She learned that if she put herself down first, it meant that others wouldn't have the chance. While she didn't like the way she felt in either case, it was less painful to devalue herself than to risk being devalued by others.

Once Patricia connected the dots between her present-day behavior and the way she had been treated in childhood, she was able to forge ahead on a new path. Patricia learned how to validate herself by practicing the art of compassionate self-affirmation. She stopped letting those who worked for her disregard the guidelines she set for them. She finally came to trust in her own capacities as a manager.

Josie, on the other hand, camouflaged a very poor self-image by becoming an arrogant know-it-all around her coworkers. She routinely put others down and couldn't handle it if they were given kudos for their good work. While she was highly successful in the creative arts field, deep down she felt like an imposter. While her protective defense (arrogance) shielded her from consciously feeling her shame, it also kept her from having positive relationships with other people.

Josie had internalized the message in childhood that any display of softness or vulnerability would be viewed as a weakness and would leave her open to attack from others. Josie had been a very loving and sensitive child, but in order to survive her environment, she needed to develop a defense to keep from getting hurt. Josie acted like she was better than everyone else so that others couldn't see her sense of weakness. But, on some level, she always knew she was pretending.

Josie needed to make room for all of her needs and emotions. She needed to embrace the fact that having feelings made her human, not inadequate. Once she interrupted her shame spiral, she could then proceed with the steps she needed to take toward healthy interactions with others. Eventually her relationships improved considerably. Once she embraced her own tenderness, she actually became the person in the office who people most commonly sought out for advice and assistance.

Stop for a moment and think about ways in which you might be shaming yourself. Use the following checklist to see whether you suffer from shame but don't even know it. There are the obvious ways to spot shame problems, such as low self-esteem, getting easily embarrassed, not liking yourself, and putting yourself down. But there are many less obvious traits that also suggest shame may be lurking. Some of these are:

- Difficulty looking people in the eyes while communicating
- Believing that other's needs are more important than your own
- Tendency to put down your accomplishments or successes
- Constantly thinking and talking about yourself in negative terms
- Fear that others will discover you are not as competent as you try to appear
- Quickness to become defensive if someone offers constructive criticism
- Feeling entitled to more than your fair share
- Unwillingness to ask for help when needed.

For now, just notice if any of these describe you. And ask your-self, "Are there any other ways that I manifest shame?" If so, make a list of them. You will find exercises and tools that will help you overcome shame throughout this book.

## Procrastination

Procrastination, the other most common roadblock to change, is the act of postponing what could and should be done now. I think if we're honest, we probably all have experienced at least a few oc-casions of procrastination. But this can become quite an obstacle if it's a chronic problem.

Procrastination is not the same as delaying a project or a goal because of an unforeseen circumstance. It's not laziness, either. Rather, it's a pattern of avoiding things that make us emotionally uncomfortable.

People procrastinate for all kinds of reasons. Those reasons usually aren't obvious or rational, and often they're fear-based. Some of the reasons we procrastinate include:

- Fear of doing a task incorrectly and receiving disapproval
- Fear of acknowledging that you really don't want to do something you have committed to doing
- Not knowing how to say "no"
- Putting more on your plate than you could possibly accomplish
- Not taking seriously the things you commit to doing.

Samantha, a forty-year-old accountant, worked for a very flex-ible firm. Her company held the philosophy that it's best to refrain from watching over their employees' shoulders while they worked, and instead gave them a lot of slack to do their jobs. Of course, if they didn't complete what was expected of them on a regular basis, they would be reprimanded or fired.

Samantha was in heaven when she found this job. She loved the freedom she was given. She could finally create her own schedule and not have anyone pestering her about what she was doing. She knew her deadlines, and she could implement any method she needed in order to meet them, just as long as she did in fact meet them. Samantha, however, was a procrastinator. Hence, what could have been a very laid-back job with great perks actually turned out to be a nightmare with tremendously high stress because Samantha constantly waited until the last minute before frantically working overtime to get her tasks done.

While Samantha truly loved the fact that she didn't have to answer to anyone on a regular basis, she didn't have the tools to handle the freedom. Because of her tendency to procrastinate, she had unconsciously set herself up to be on edge. She could never relax because she feared getting fired for missing her deadlines.

As a child, Samantha's dad told her she was lazy and that she would never amount to anything. While Samantha was kind of a laid-back child who liked to do things at a slower pace than other kids, she certainly wasn't lazy. However, because of the negative messages she had internalized, she began to fulfill this prophecy, and she appeared to become lazier and lazier as she approached adolescence.

However, Samantha was certainly very capable, and she also really wanted approval from her parents. Unknowingly, however, she created a personal system of behavior where she would wait until the very last minute and then put all of her energy into whatever she was expected to complete, like school work or chores. Amazingly, she would then manage to get it all together in record time. But she had become conditioned to respond to all of her responsibilities in crisis-like terms. While in some ways she looked like a star because of how quickly she could get things done, she suffered a huge downside in terms of the internal stress that this behavior caused her. Plus, she could never fully enjoy her downtime because she was perpetually worried about getting things finished.

Samantha's tendency to push things off also affected her workplace relationships. She was frequently unable to attend company events or socialize with her colleagues because of her deadline pressures. And her coworkers responded negatively to her constant anxiety. Fortunately, by working through her old stuff, Samantha eventually discovered that by letting go of the internalized negative messages, she no longer needed to sabotage her success. She learned to work at a steadier pace, lost her anxiety over getting fired, and even used her abundance of extra energy to take up skiing and tennis.

▸ *Procrastination Exercise*

Do you struggle with procrastination? If so, look back in your childhood to try to discover the roots. If you can't find the missing pieces to the puzzle, don't worry. The key is to recognize that you are sabotaging yourself and to find a new way of behaving. Acknowledge to yourself that though you first learned to procrastinate for a good reason, it is no longer useful for your current mission to improve your workplace relationships. Forgive yourself for it. Then challenge yourself to set up a priority list and stick to it. Always give yourself permission to readjust your priorities if what you've decided doesn't actually work for you.

In addition to identifying the roadblocks to making changes, it's also important to have a general idea of what kind of relationships you're aiming to achieve. So let's move on to learning about the qualities that distinguish good workplace relationships.

## The Qualities of Positive Workplace Relationships

Using the descriptions below to form a model of positive relationships will help you determine how much of your workplace chaos is "self-generated" rather than "other-generated." After all, as mentioned earlier, caregivers don't have a monopoly on dysfunctional behavior. Bosses, coworkers, employees, and the rest of our work gang can all behave in ways that are, objectively, intolerable or unacceptable. But their behavior often appears even more intolerable because it presses on a previously existing sore spot. Or, because of our old stuff, we may lack effective adultlike ways to handle tough relationship interactions, or we don't know how to take good care of ourselves. Having a better understanding of healthy characteristics in the workplace can help us visualize what to strive for in order to improve relationships.

Though there are many types of job relationships, for our purposes I have divided them into three main roles—the boss, the subordinate or employee, and the coworker.

## The Boss

Being the boss entails many important responsibilities and, along with them, the need to establish effective rules and policies. The key word here is "effective." Many bosses are quite skilled at defining parameters and expectations but have no idea how to implement them constructively. Others put them into action but do so in a way that's too harsh and insensitive to individual needs. These types often don't notice that they make problems worse by alienating their employees or subordinates. Still others have trouble setting any standards at all, and these tend to lose the respect of others.

Of course, all professions are not equal, and not all companies within a particular profession would operate well using only one standard. Some companies are looser and more informal than others, and different fields have very different workplace cultures. For instance, a corporation that deals with top-secret information would most likely require its engineers and managers to be far more tight-lipped and formal than would a company that builds auto parts for standard domestic vehicles. A charge nurse in a small community hospital may do fine by being more informal with her staff than a charge nurse at a hospital that treats prison inmates. Hence, the guideline for setting good boundaries needs to be adapted to the specific climate of the company.

Although the requirements of being a competent boss (especially when it comes to creating a positive atmosphere) will differ across companies and professions, there are some basic characteristics applicable to all. Bosses should at minimum provide employees with the following:

- A clear description outlining very specifically the tasks expected to be performed, as well as how they are to be completed
- Descriptions of each position in the team, department, or company (depending on the organization's size) so that everyone has a clear picture of each person's responsibilities
- Timelines for each task or project
- Clear policies regarding dress code, consequences for tardiness, vacation and personal time, and office comportment
- Policies regarding social/personal relationships and harassment between subordinates and superiors, or among coworkers
- Policies regarding compensation, including overtime compensation.

In addition to providing appropriate job descriptions and workplace policies, employers should be respectful of their employees' time. Responsible employers don't exploit their employees. They do not expect more from them than they have outlined in their written description, at least not without proper compensation. They treat all employees fairly, and they do not have inappropriate relationships with subordinates. They understand the realm of their power and never abuse it. For example, they do not take advantage of those who admire or look up to them as mentors.

While many bosses love having overzealous employees who are always willing to go the extra mile and expect nothing in return but a pat on the back, the healthy bosses makes sure to compensate these individuals with either more money, extra time off, or other appropriate rewards. Of course, it's always best for an employee to take responsibility for caring for herself and make sure that she doesn't let a boss take advantage of her. But it's also the employer's responsibility to make sure not to cross these boundaries.

Peter, the CEO of a large company, took great pride in the fact that the bulk of his employees didn't take all of their vacation time, and many of them would spend several hours a week beyond their salary compensation to get a very large workload completed. Unbeknownst to Peter, many of his employees were in competition with each other to be seen as the most-prized employee. Because Peter believed that a worker who would dedicate her whole life to the job was the most valuable worker, he paid little attention or respect to those employees who did a good job but who also had interests outside the workplace. What Peter didn't realize was that his employees were actually afraid of him.

Peter had been solely valued for his achievements as a child. His parents were constantly on the go, never stopping to smell the roses and enjoy life. Hence, Peter never learned the value of play and leisure time.

Peter's employees feared that they might be fired if they were to actually ask for any much-needed time off to rejuvenate and to be able to give their best efforts to the job. But once Peter learned that he was continuing to re-create his old vulnerabilities in the workplace, imposing the unrealistic expectation his parents had of him onto his employees, he was able to create an environment in which people truly *wanted* to come to work.

Peter began offering flextime to employees who were new parents. He made sure that everyone took their earned vacation time, and he no longer held in highest regard those employee who had no life other than work. Rather, he encouraged everyone at the company to maintain a balanced existence. Lo and behold, the company's productivity increased! Of course, we can't all expect our bosses to have the kind of epiphany that Peter experienced, but it's still important to strive to situate ourselves in workplace environments that support our growth and offer us respect.

Just as it is important for supervisors and managers not to exploit others, it's equally important that staff and employees not take advantage of their bosses. Many bosses also have old emotional baggage. They can be just as afraid of disapproval or of not being liked as are the people who work for them. These bosses fail to set appropriate boundaries, and their employees constantly take advantage of them. While it's great for bosses to be compassionate and understanding of their employees' needs, it's not a boss's job to be a parent, a spouse, or even a friend. In order for workplace relationships to be healthy, both the bosses and the employees need to get their personal needs met elsewhere.

Nicole, the vice president of a marketing firm, grew up in a very chaotic home in which her caregivers verbally abused her, her older brother picked on her, and her older sister perceived her to be a "big pest." Nicole coped with her emotional bruising by making herself extremely likable to everyone. Unfortunately, this led her to become like a chameleon, someone who would adjust her identity to become whatever she thought others expected her to be.

In some ways this quality served Nicole very well, because it helped her to climb the ranks at her job. But while she got several promotions because of her endearing nature, she never developed the ability to say "no," to be assertive, or to deal with conflict. For this she had paid a very high price: as she had advanced in her career, she had been sexually harassed by several male executives. Plus, once Nicole was put in charge of other employees, she was so fearful of stepping on other people's toes and possibly hurting their feelings that she couldn't do what was necessary to manage her staff.

In our work together, Nicole learned to understand that she was no longer the child who feared she would be abandoned for asserting her rights to say "no" to mistreatment. She recognized that as an adult she was no longer so dependent on others, and that she could give herself the approval and respect she desperately sought from those around her. This awareness gave her the strength and confidence necessary to assert herself with her staff (as well as her bosses) and to get her job done effectively.

Even if you've successfully managed to heal your old bruises, if you're in a position of power, you need to understand the dynamics of people in less powerful positions, since you're very likely to encounter other people who continue to have their emotional leftovers wreaking havoc in the workplace. And, because many people don't get the help they need and deserve, as a boss, you need to recognize how these issues might play out in your interactions with them.

With this understanding, you will become more centered and less reactive. Plus, it will make your job a whole lot easier. So please, make sure to also read the next section.

## The Employee

If you work for someone else, your freedom to make decisions is clearly more limited than if you are the boss. But this doesn't necessarily have to be a bad thing. Most people who earn a living do so by working for someone else. But for many, it's hard to make peace with the fact that someone else runs the show.

Many people attempt to control things they have no control over. They put their energy in wrong directions, trying to fix problems that are outside their control. Remember Darcy, from Chapter Two? Before she healed her bruises, she was consumed with the behavior of her boss rather than looking at the ways she could improve her own situation. She wasn't fully taking responsibility for her own actions or responses.

Many people with old bruises burden themselves with stuff they can't control, like their reactions to other people's behavior, feelings, or thoughts. This often means they don't have enough energy to take charge of the things that are within their own power to control, like their *own* behavior and feelings. At the same time they tend to seek approval from others, often at the expense of doing what they truly think is best for themselves. They often sabotage their own success by passively rebelling against things they perceive as unjust or unreasonable. Rather than voice their thoughts directly, they may show up late or do a sloppy job on a project they've been assigned. They act childishly, forgetting that as adults they now have choices they may not have had in childhood. Hence, having to follow rules and guidelines set by others can be very difficult for those who remain stuck in their old stuff.

Cynthia's biggest childhood hurt was that she felt she didn't get her fair share of love and acceptance from her family. She felt that her brother and two sisters were treated more kindly and were generally better liked than she was.

In adulthood, Cynthia hadn't come to recognize that she had many direct avenues she could pursue in order to get her needs met. For instance, she believed she was being mistreated on the job, but she didn't feel entitled to stand up for herself. When she did occasionally assert her needs, she didn't know how to do so effectively. Often, she would become demanding, resembling a three-year-old having a tantrum.

Cynthia had no idea that she could directly address her boss, or that she could write a letter specifying the problem. Because she couldn't grasp her adult choices, she further disintegrated into childlike behavior by sneaking out early, not completing her tasks on time, and not taking responsibility for her mistakes. Or sometimes, when she couldn't take her boss anymore, she would have verbal outbursts. These sabotaging behaviors (byproducts of her unhealed stuff) eventually got her fired.

Working for someone doesn't have to be problematic. In fact, people who have learned appropriate ways to satisfy their own previously unmet needs can have positive experiences with authority figures. They can thrive despite the drama that surrounds them.

To have a positive workplace experience as an employee, you need to begin practicing the following guidelines:

- Resolve any issues you might have related to following your workplace's rules. Don't make excuses for your behavior if you have violated company policy—either stop behaving outside of the bounds or accept full responsibility when you fail to meet the requirements
- Wholeheartedly accept your position as an employee for as long as you are choosing to work for someone else
- If you decide you're not comfortable working for someone else, strive to become self-employed
- Claim your job as something you are *choosing* to do, not something you *have* to do
- Develop reasonable expectations of your boss, getting rid of any needs for him or her to fulfill the role of parent, friend, or spouse

- Learn how to assert yourself clearly without being defensive, harsh, or demanding
- Treat yourself with respect, so that others won't have any other choice but to treat you in kind.

Of course, if you don't know how to put all of these guidelines into practice as of yet, that's certainly understandable. Through the course of this book, you'll be supplied with many tools that will make it much easier for you to follow these guidelines.

Also, please note that if you work for a boss of your same gender, you might be prone to expecting greater understanding and compassion, believing that certain boundaries don't need to be present once the gender barrier is removed. If so, let me caution you to think again. In the workplace, our expectations and standards of behavior should not be biased by gender. A boss is a boss, and an employee is an employee. Treating each other as humans with unique personalities and sensitivities, rather than as males or females, can help all of us get rid of unrealistic expectations for special treatment.

## The Coworker

Our relationships with our peers in the workplace can be very tricky. While coworker relationships are the most equal in status, if we have unhealed bruises, these relationships can become just as problematic as the ones with our bosses or our subordinates. If we're not aware of our problematic stuff, we will unknowingly set up dynamics that could repeat the kinds of hurts experienced in childhood.

Karen had a very contentious and competitive relationship with her older sister, Jane, and she had never spent the time or energy necessary to deal with the fallout from their negative relationship. Even as adults, Karen and Jane rarely spoke to one another. And when they did, they usually ended up in a fight, unable to resolve their conflicts.

Karen worked for a large clothing manufacturer, where she was required to work in very close, cooperative proximity to her peers. Karen quickly befriended one of her coworkers, Sarah. They joked around a lot and made each other laugh. They seemed to have a lot in common.

However, not long after they'd begun their workplace "friendship," they started quarrelling and becoming competitive. Karen hadn't noticed before that Sarah had many of the same qualities as Jane—they were both loud, boisterous, and fairly aggressive. While these qualities appealed to Karen initially, they made her edgy and uncomfortable once her relationship with Sarah became closer.

Karen grew to become very resentful of Sarah and to regret that she'd trusted her. She even felt a sense of betrayal. In reality, Sarah really never did anything to deceive or betray Karen. It turned out that Karen was drawn to befriend Sarah precisely because Sarah reminded her of Jane. What Karen didn't realize was that by befriending Sarah, she was seeking to repair her feelings for her sister through this new relationship. But she didn't have the tools to maintain a relationship with Sarah because she had never healed her bruised feelings regarding Jane.

Of course it's true that many people we encounter in the workplace might not be the nicest people we know, or the ones with whom we'd choose to become close. But oftentimes, because of our old unhealed stuff, we are actually viewing these people through the eyes of a bruised child. Even though we're actually on par with them, professionally, we don't experience ourselves as on the same level playing field. Because of the inhibitions caused by our unhealed stuff, we give away all of our personal power and control, and we end up feeling victimized by others' behavior. Sure, many of our coworkers may have annoying characteristics, but the fact that we let these bother us so much usually has something to do with unfinished business we have with someone else.

Emotionally healthy people are those who develop the ability to distinguish among their coworkers those who are truly malicious from those who simply push their buttons—that is, their old vulnerabilities. Once we heal our old bruises, we stop having these same problematic reactions to these people.

Catherine was dumped by her high-school sweetheart when she was sixteen. She didn't have personal resources at the time to mend her broken heart. Instead, she tried to brush it off as no big deal. But she was never the same again. In particular, she internalized a negative view of men as "heartbreakers." Unconsciously, she resolved never to get truly close to a guy again.

What Catherine failed to realize was that this kind of incomplete resolution would continue to affect other aspects of her life—even her work life. Joe, whom Catherine started working with years later, resembled her high-school sweetheart. He was kind and easy to work with. Catherine found herself very attracted to Joe. However, because of Catherine's old bruise, she distrusted Joe. Without his ever showing any real signs that he couldn't be trusted, Catherine started treating Joe like the "jerk" who had dumped her. She expressed her conflicted, negative feelings about Joe by picking on him and teasing him, causing him to file a formal complaint against her with their company.

Healthy coworker relationships require that we heal our old bruises so that we don't slop this old stuff onto innocent others the way Catherine did with Joe. Plus, while there is nothing inherently wrong with our developing friendships with our coworkers (as long as there is nothing exploitative in those relationships), we should always proceed cautiously. As a general rule, the more we blur professional boundaries by becoming more personal with our workplace peers, the higher the chances of resulting painful drama. Thus, we need to understand very clearly what we stand to gain and what we stand to lose by making a coworker relationship into a more personal one.

Of course, many of us have developed some of our most important friendships in the workplace, as this is often one of the best ways we have to meet new people. But we need to create these bonds responsibly. If we do develop a friendship with a coworker, we must take pains to keep the professional aspect of that relationship separate and distinct, and not allow personal issues to intrude in the workplace. We all have to spend a great deal of time in our coworkers' presence. It serves us best to learn the boundaries that make these relationships as effective and comfortable as possible.

The following guidelines will help you establish healthy boundaries with coworkers:

- Keep personal business outside of your relationships with coworkers.
- If you have an established friendship with a coworker, take pains to remind yourself that while you're both on the job, a coworker should be treated like a coworker and not like a friend. Recognize the different responsibilities and limits involved in the workplace setting.
- Follow all of your company's protocols for handling conflicts with coworkers.
- Be responsible for your part in any interactions you have with your coworkers, whether they're positive or negative.
- Always treat your coworkers with respect.

In general, if you have a history of conflicts with your coworkers, there's a really good chance that you are bringing your old issues to the mix. But if you don't tend to have conflicts with coworkers, but then find yourself at odds with a coworker who *does* tend to have problems with peers, then there's a good chance it's this coworker who is bringing the unresolved issues to the mix. In these situations, there's still a risk that you are letting this problem coworker press your buttons.

Always look at your own role in how you might be adding to the problem, and try to avoid pointing the finger and blaming others. As they say, "it takes two to tango." I have almost always found this to be the case in relationships where both people have equal power and workplace standing.

▶ *Inventory Exercise*

Becoming emotionally healthy will allow you to develop the most effective and most appropriate workplace relationships. But before moving on to the actual eight steps, take a look at your relationships using the above descriptions as a guideline. Make a list of the areas where you think you might have difficulties. See if there are any patterns that have followed you throughout your past workplace situations. Patterns are a pretty good indicator that it's our own issue, not someone else's problem. This will help you focus your efforts on what's most relevant to your life.

As you go through your own inventory, be careful not to shame yourself for any of it. Remember that the only chance we have of making something work better in our lives is to understand what isn't working, while understanding that its existence did have a purpose at some earlier point in time. When we stop shaming and blaming, we can start taking responsibility and begin thriving.

► *Four*

# Befriend Your Emotional Bruises

What a concept! Making friends with the old stuff that still pains you. I wouldn't doubt it if you were asking yourself, "Is she out of her mind?" If so, don't worry. This concept isn't as strange as it sounds. Just continue reading. I'm pretty sure you'll soon understand how important this step is to the process of eliminating workplace drama.

Creating fulfilling workplace relationships with our bosses and coworkers (not to mention with our lovers, friends, and family) requires an in-depth understanding *and* appreciation of who we are as individuals. And in order to become this self-aware, we must master many challenges. Basically we need to be able to do all of the following:

- Distinguish what we like from what we don't like.
- Understand what our values are and where they come from.
- Adjust our behavior and responses to the demands of our present lives, and leave behind any old patterns of thinking or behaving that don't work well in our current environment.
- Establish a framework for the things about ourselves that we're willing to compromise on and those things we won't or cannot change.

Unfortunately, many people haven't realized that if they have any leftover bruises or hurts that have been pushed out of their conscious awareness—denied, ignored, buried, or blocked—they'll never be able to take charge of their experience in the workplace, let alone find the fulfillment they crave. Rather, they'll remain trapped in a prison of ineffective coping strategies and rigid defenses. They might be able to survive and even get ahead, but they'll never really be free to thrive.

Granted, for some of us it may be a treacherous challenge to dig up buried hurts. But there's no way around it. If old bruises like these exist, whether we're conscious of them or not, they will drain our energy in the present. Thus, we simply must be willing to go on this treasure hunt before we can ever possibly achieve the fulfillment we all deserve. And the place to start is by understanding and embracing our vulnerabilities.

Of course, all of this is much easier said than done. And, if you're anything like the person I was in my own early adulthood, you might be highly skeptical as to whether these things are actually within your own control anyway. You might be asking, "How does someone ever achieve this kind of balance?" Or you might be rolling your eyes and saying, "Yeah, right—in an ideal world maybe, but I'll never achieve this because I work for (or with) a bunch of nuts." Well, rest assured. It doesn't matter who you work for, or who you work with. *You* have the power to improve your workplace experience.

Of course, I certainly appreciate how the idea of befriending emotional bruises might strike you as odd or even silly, especially if you've been taught to pick yourself up by your bootstraps and carry on despite any adversity you might have endured. I used to wholeheartedly believe that whatever hurt feelings I had left over from childhood should be ignored. In fact, I believed that even acknowledging any old bruises would be a sign of weakness. I quickly came to realize that I wasn't alone in this thinking.

Many of the people I've worked with over the years came into therapy initially reporting that they had had the "perfect childhood." But they were also letting me know that their lives were a mess in the present, both personally and professionally. They had no explanations for this discrepancy other than things like, "I've been a victim of bad luck," or, "I just keep getting involved with bad people." I saw that it was even more common for people who felt their childhood had been pretty rosy to explain their adult unhappiness as a byproduct of their being a "failure" or an "idiot." These people embarked on the therapy process seeing themselves as powerless, without choices. They couldn't even fathom the concept that maybe they were still bogged down by unresolved issues stemming from a long time ago.

For many, the links simply weren't apparent, or else they'd never been taught to believe that any connections between their childhoods and their adulthood experiences could exist. Or if they acknowledged that there could be a link in the abstract, they were too embarrassed to apply this principle specifically to their own lives. Some would say things like, "Sure, so-and-so had it really bad. Of course, it makes sense that she would be a mess now," when describing a friend's problems. Others were curious about understanding the link between childhood hurts and problems in their *intimate* relationships, but they remained reluctant to believe that the same connection could also apply to *workplace* relationships.

It would often take months for these highly intelligent, resourceful individuals to grasp the notion that at least some of their current woes were directly related to buried bruises—that is, to having ignored feelings of sadness, hurt, or anger stemming from their not having gotten some of their important needs met as children. This recognition was especially difficult for those who had not endured any blatant abuse or neglect, as described in Chapter One. Plus, they certainly didn't want to "blame" anyone for their current suffering. Thus, the only option they saw was to deny that they even had any leftover emotional stuff to begin with.

Fortunately, after some gentle coaching from me, they came to recognize that as children they had been *dependent* on others for their care, just like all of us were when we were kids, and that it was their adult caregivers who had borne the responsibility for nurturing their emotional well-being while they were growing. By realizing the limits of their own responsibility during childhood, they were able to open the door to revisit their earlier experiences with more compassion and understanding.

Please take note that compassion toward yourself for having experienced emotional distress doesn't let you off the hook for being accountable for your own behavior in adulthood. The formula for becoming happy starts with claiming full responsibility for your own choices, taking full charge of the things you have control over, and letting go of those things that you can't control. However, compassion, understanding, kindness, empathy—all of these qualities help to free you from shame and self-blame, so that the challenge of self-accountability and responsibility becomes much more doable. We'll focus more on the importance of responsibility in the next chapter. For now, let's keep our attention on how to develop the compassion you need in order to befriend your old bruises.

Despite our common tendency to shove away or bury old stuff, try to resist. I can't emphasize enough how important it is both to recognize and to admit the fallout from whatever emotional bruises, big or small, remain unhealed. Otherwise these will continue to interfere with your goal of creating positive workplace relationships. Time and time again, experience has taught me that unhealed stuff will inevitably get best of us, surfacing at the most inopportune times.

## There Is No Perfect Childhood

Always keep in mind that *everyone* has had experiences during their formative years that have caused, at the very least, some minor emotional bruising. *No one has had the perfect childhood.* It's simply not possible—no parent or other important caregiver can ever fully address a child's every need, nor can society ever meet all of the needs of every individual within it. Besides, even the most idyllic childhood can result in a limited capacity to handle complex or difficult people and situations. In other words, even those born with a silver spoon in their mouths, and an abundance of love surrounding them, often grow up emotionally challenged when it comes to dealing with disappointments, conflict, and life's inevitable hardships. Believe it or not, the absence of adversity can truly be a disadvantage in adulthood. Of course, if you are among the more fortunate, your scars may have either faded altogether (because of good support and nurturance from friends, family, or a therapist) or the bruises were never that bad to begin with. If so, then quite possibly you may not have as much digging to do. But for many far less fortunate, these emotional aches continue to beg for attention and repair.

Nancy, a thirtysomething public official, couldn't grasp the idea that her upbringing by a hysterical, excessively self-centered father and an emotionally unavailable mother had anything to do with the unbearable relationship she was experiencing with her boss. She and her boss were in constant turmoil: he had unrealistic expectations of her performance, and she had no ability to set appropriate boundaries with him. How was it possible that her childlike responses to her boss were directly linked to having felt cheated out of appropriate love and attention in her youth? After all, she hadn't been under her parents' roof for years!

Unbeknownst to Nancy, she couldn't take a self-respecting adult stance toward her boss because she was still hurt by the constant disapproval and lack of regard she had received from her parents. She had become stuck in a vicious cycle of needing her boss to address the pain that came from this bruise by giving Nancy accolades and appreciating her hard work. What she couldn't see was that her boss presented her with a set of emotional issues that were very similar to those presented to her as a child by her mom and dad.

Nancy was so caught up in her own despair that she couldn't see that her boss had his own deficiencies. She was blind to the fact that he couldn't possibly give her what she deserved, such as pats on the back and a realistic appraisal of her good work. She couldn't grasp that she would never be able to please him, and that going to someone like him for approval was like going to the hardware store for groceries: at best, she might end up with a small snack like a candy bar or some peanuts, but hardly enough to fix a nutritious meal. Fortunately, by understanding how her old bruises came into play, Nancy eventually saw the light in terms of how to handle her boss. Most important of all, she learned that she had the option to leave her job, or else give up this need to have her boss praise her work.

Once Nancy embraced her choices, she no longer related to her boss as her parent. And she took much better care of herself in the workplace. She stopped working overtime without compensation, and she became okay with the fact that her boss would be perpetually unhappy with her. She stopped feeling sorry for herself. And she began cultivating friendships with people outside the workplace who were capable of providing the emotional support she needed. Plus, by taking more responsibility for herself and changing her expectations of her boss, she also became a much better supervisor to her own subordinates—she was far less stressed and more easygoing.

## Don't Compare

Of course, you may have had it much worse than Nancy did, or maybe not so bad at all. Regardless, it's very important that you *don't compare*. Instead, focus on the importance of your *own* experience and your *own* desire to break free from destructive patterns. Also, to ease any overwhelming sense that you're just now realizing that your closet is filled with ugly rags, keep in mind that what we're doing here is not meant to be a witch-hunt. You won't be asked to confront anyone from your past who you feel had wronged or hurt you, either intentionally or unintentionally. But you will be asked to open your mind and heart to understanding where and how you were bruised, and to entertain the possibility that your leftover stuff isn't an enemy that needs to be shut out.

Also, keep in mind that many people developed emotional tender spots because they didn't *register* enough of the right kind of love and nurturance from the people who cared for them. I emphasize "register" because you might be resistant to making a connection between your workplace struggles in the present and how you were treated as a kid because you believe you actually had a pretty good childhood. The key is to realize that it's possible that the goods didn't get fully internalized. If so, you can still cut people slack who were generally good caregivers, while at the same time acknowledging whatever happened that didn't fit right for your development.

A failure to register love, respect, and care can occur because a caregiver really missed the boat in providing adequate protection, love, and limits. But it can also occur because the child couldn't accept or absorb those qualities due to her temperament or other developmental difficulties. Remember, even though children are not responsible for their own care (rather, their caregivers are responsible), this doesn't always mean that caregivers were objectively inadequate or bad. They may have been great people but unaware of how exactly to fulfill the unique needs of the children for whom they cared.

Most importantly, however, for our concerns in the present, it's important to understand that it doesn't really matter whether your parents or other caregivers were truly wonderful, or whether they were inadequate or neglectful, or whether they were a combination. If you were hurt—whether you remember it or not, or whether the bruises were intentionally or unintentionally inflicted, or whether they were big or small—your body and mind have had to cope with the resulting pain. And until you identify, acknowledge, and heal this pain, it will continue to affect you in the present.

### Imagery

In case you're having trouble digesting the idea that your emotional pain counts no matter how great it is or where it came from, consider the following situation. If you are leaving my office and I break your arm accidentally because I wasn't paying attention when I closed the door, does your arm need medical attention? Is it any less broken because I didn't mean to hurt you? Does it need any less medical treatment because it was an accident? You know where I'm going, right? In essence, our emotional selves require the same kind of care as our physical bodies. So try to refrain from making excuses for other people's behavior, and don't brainwash yourself into believing that your pain doesn't count.

Of course, acknowledging your bruises and being compassionate toward yourself for your pain doesn't let you off the hook for taking responsibility for yourself today. In fact, the whole premise of this book is to help you take full responsibility for your own emotional life and the choices you make in your workplace relationships. Paradoxically, by befriending your old stuff (the origins of which you weren't responsible for), you pave the way for having the energy and ability to fully claim your adult status.

Take a moment now to clear out any shame or embarrassment. As you recall from the previous chapter, too much shame is the biggest obstacle to progress and change. So be very careful not to burden yourself with any thoughts that you are a freak, or an idiot, or an emotional cripple because you have been affected by your childhood experiences. You are in good company. Everyone is a product of the sum total and interaction of all their prior experiences and perceptions of those experiences. Everyone has been emotionally bruised to some degree in childhood. That's just part of the imperfect nature of life.

Now, let's move on to understanding the various defense mechanisms you may have employed in childhood to help lessen the blows to your developing self-identity.

## Defense Mechanisms

Whatever caused our bruises, we are instinctually driven to avoid feeling pain and hurt. Just as we are wired to pull our hand away from a hot stove as quickly as we register the heat, we also reflexively try to protect ourselves from emotions we find too painful to tolerate. Hence, whether consciously or not, we create all kinds of clever ways to feel better. We might hide, flee, or fight. Or we might deceive, ignore, manipulate, or minimize. We employ these defenses to protect us from feeling too much pain.

Granted, some people have somehow lived in their pain without defenses. They haven't erected any mechanisms for self-protection. These people are often seen as the "walking wounded." Unfortunately, many such people have enormous difficulty surviving at all, often resorting to forms of self-mutilation or even suicide attempts. If this describes you, then please seek other assistance as well. This book may offer you some useful insights and tools, but you will most likely need much more help and support for your healing.

Fortunately, most of us have gotten enough love, support, and affirmation along the way to ensure that we haven't grown up to be totally defenseless. Most of us have managed to form some protective mechanisms that allow us to bracket off, at least to some degree, our emotional bruises in order to get by in the workplace.

Defense mechanisms come in many forms. But because children's resources are limited, they can only be as clever as their emotional development permits. Whereas in adulthood we have an abundance of choices and opportunities to handle situations (even the painful ones), children are stuck with only a few options at best. As a result, many of the means to feel better that we developed in our youth won't be very effective in our adulthood. In fact, they might even cost us our jobs.

Consider Stella, a twenty-six-year-old employee of a large pharmaceutical company, who had learned early that it wasn't safe to express her creativity and intelligence around her mother, Barbara. Tragically, she learned to dumb herself down to not threaten her mother's self-esteem. Barbara had dropped out of college when she became pregnant and never returned to finish her degree. Though Barbara would never admit it, Stella sensed that her mom resented her, and she feared Barbara would be angry enough to reject her if Stella were to ever outshine her. To cope with this dreadful dynamic of feeling compelled to protect her mother from feeling bad about herself, Stella unknowingly had convinced herself that her own drive for success really wasn't all that important.

As you can well imagine, Stella paid a pretty high price for this unconscious deal she had made with her emotions. She had tremendous difficulty letting herself excel in the workplace because she feared her boss would be threatened by her contributions. So she would sabotage her successes by turning her assignments in late, and her work was of a quality that was clearly far beneath her full potential.

Stella's situation illustrates how many of the ways we learned to cope with our lives as children no longer serve us well as adults, especially in the workplace. In fact, many of these mechanisms actually interfere with our achieving our goals and having positive interactions with others. Nevertheless, these defenses stick around in adulthood because they become habits.

Let's take a look at these different kinds of defenses and how they affect us in the workplace. Then we will look at what lies beneath them—yes, those emotional bruises. Of course, none of us likes to look at the darker sides of ourselves. And our defenses aren't always pretty. If fact, some of them can be downright abusive. As we look at them, you might be tempted to dismiss them prematurely as not being descriptive of your own behavior. But if you recognize that your admission and acceptance puts you on the road to achieving your aims of greater satisfaction, better workplace relationships, less conflict, and increased productivity, you might find it a bit easier to face your challenges head on and ultimately put yourself back in charge of your choices.

Of course, many of these common defenses listed below won't apply to you, but I'm fairly certain that you will have witnessed some or many of these behaviors in your coworkers, bosses, and employees. After all, they're human too, subject to the same influences as you were from your childhood. So by learning more about these defense mechanisms, you'll not only get a better handle on what's driving your own behavior, but also become better equipped to handle other people's workplace behavior too.

I've given these defense mechanisms humorous labels in an attempt to make them easier to understand and, I hope, less shamebound. As you review the following list, pay close attention to whether you or someone you work with fits the description. Try not to be judgmental. Just notice and acknowledge what fits.

1. **The Hot Potato:** You've learned to keep tossing uncomfortable things into the hands of others. Clearly, we all toss the potato from time to time by blaming someone else for our mistakes or by denying reality, especially when we are too ashamed to admit something. But if this has become your dominant mode in relationships, you're going to have problems. Accepting responsibility for your own behavior becomes a burden—most likely because you've already had to take on far more than your fair share to begin with. This defense often emerges in people who were blamed for things that were ultimately their caregivers' responsibility.

2. **The Einstein:** You've learned to protect yourself from your inner emotional life by intellectualizing everything, most likely at a high cost to your passion and vibrancy. When asked how you *feel*, you report what you *think*. In the workplace, people may perceive you as arrogant. You may not mean to seem superior, and may not see yourself as such, but you may be giving this sense to others, and they may feel threatened by you. Again, while this demeanor may have been necessary or useful when you were a child, it's bound to lead to some difficulties with your getting along with coworkers. This defense is common among people who come from families where emotions are devalued or not understood.

3. **The Turtle:** A hard shell is an excellent resource when you truly need to hide, but not so good when a situation requires your full involvement. This defense is often developed by people who have been abused psychologically or physically, or who witnessed others being mistreated. It allows you to convince yourself that if you don't see it, then it didn't happen. For instance, Peter's parents were violent toward each other, often in front of him. When these altercations took place, Peter would be coached afterward either by his mom or his dad that he must never tell anyone what he witnessed,

in order to protect the family's reputation. Over the years, it became torturous for him to keep quiet. So, in order to manage this impossible situation, he learned to tune out the violence by disconnecting with reality. He would instead hide in fantasy so he wouldn't have to face the ugliness around him. As an adult, in the workplace, Peter had difficulty dealing with even the slightest turmoil or conflict, whether involving himself or between others.

4. **The Wounded Bird:** This may not seem like a defense at all. In fact, Wounded Birds often appear so vulnerable and raw that other people are afraid to approach them. This defense requires other people to either walk on eggshells or to be extra kind and sensitive to the Wounded Birds' feelings, thus protecting them from even deeper wounds. The Wounded Bird looks like a victim, and as a result other people feel sorry for her. Those who use this defense often put themselves down, publicly shaming themselves so that others can't squash them first. This defense is also common to those who were badly treated as children and learned to enlist sympathy in order to get any of their emotional needs met.

5. **The Big Shot/Bully:** You put out the message, "I'm stronger and fiercer than everyone else, so therefore no one can hurt me." Contrary to the common perception of bullies, they aren't always violent. Often, they appear calm and subdued, but they inflict their damage with words. People prone to behaving this way were often bullied themselves as children—though this should never be used as an excuse to rationalize bullying others. Rather than deal with the pain of having been mistreated, they find it easier and less painful to take out their pain and aggression on others. But unlike the Wounded Bird, which tends to elicit sympathy, this defense tends to frighten or anger people and keep them at arm's length. As you can understand, that's

not a very effective method of relating to others in the workplace.

6. **The Sunshine Maker:** You tend to turn even the worst negative situation into something positive. Now, don't get me wrong, I'm certainly not opposed to turning lemons into lemonade. In fact, that's what thrivers do. But the Sunshine Maker tends to do this reflexively, even prematurely, without ever really feeling anything. In the workplace, someone who uses this defense is likely to gloss over problems automatically, even serious ones that require attention. Many people prone to using this defense may have been raised by an alcoholic parent, or by someone with a debilitating illness.

Most of us use a combination of these defenses, depending on which of our buttons are being pushed. And there's a good chance that I've missed a dynamic or two that you've used at one time or else witnessed in someone else's behavior. Don't dismiss your own observations. You're the best judge of your experience.

▶ *Defense Mechanism Exercise*

Using the above listing of defenses as a guide, go back and identify which defense(s) best describe you. You might also wish to review these in terms of how they apply to the people in your workplace. When you have a moment, write down some examples from your own life when you may have used any of these defenses, either in childhood or in adulthood. Can you think of any other ways you have learned to defend yourself from old emotional pain? If so, write about them; try describing them and give them a fun label. The more you make this material useful and alive, the more you'll be able to make constructive changes in your life.

Once you've identified your primary defense mechanisms, start paying closer attention to how you employ them in the workplace. Over the next week or so, challenge yourself while at work to spot your defenses before they come into action. Try to notice who pushes your buttons and how they get pushed. To help you control them before they take you over, pay attention to what your body is doing. Our bodies give us lots of signals that we're about to get stirred up, such as sweaty palms, increased heart rate, shallow breathing, muscle tension, and even hot flashes.

After a week or two of observation, pay close attention to the sorts of feelings these defense mechanisms have been blocking out. Try to keep your list of feelings simple and make sure you're identifying *feelings*, not *thoughts*. As a general rule, if you describe an emotion with more than one or two words, you're most likely noting a perception or thought instead. For instance, if you say, "I *feel* like my boss is always picking on me," you're actually relaying your perception of your boss's behavior, not how you feel. So if this is what you perceive, then ask yourself, "What do I *feel* when my boss picks on me?" Then the answer would be something like "mad," "happy," "sad," "afraid," or a combination of feelings.

In order to have positive relationships and achieve your goals in the workplace you have to know who you are. This includes having full access to and understanding your emotions. When you make room for knowing how you feel, you have more control over your own behavior. Otherwise, your feelings will have a life of their own, which means they're more likely to wreak havoc and drive you to behave in destructive, unproductive ways.

For the last phase of this exercise, each time you spot a defense in action, say the following:

*Hey, thanks, defense, for showing up. You've helped me get through some pretty tough stuff in my life. I appreciate you. However, for right now I don't need your protection. You're welcome to stick around in case I need your services. But for this moment, I need to let myself experience my feelings more fully. And I'm going to allow myself to evaluate all the choices I have, and not keep myself so limited to just a few.*

I know, I know: this probably sounds really strange. "Who talks to themselves this way unless they're nuts?" you might be asking.

Well, it's okay. You're not nuts; you're just trying on new behaviors that are bound to be unfamiliar, and hence seem odd. But what the heck—after all, you're reading this book most likely because you already admit that something isn't working too well. So why not try something new? Besides, if it doesn't work, you can try something else. Feel free to modify this exercise any way that you see fit for your situation.

Keep in mind that acknowledging your feelings is *not* a license to act on them. For instance, if you are angry at your boss, you're not allowed to punch him in the nose. You simply want to notice your feelings and give them permission to be. That way you'll know better what you're dealing with, and you can make more appropriate choices according to your situation. The aim is to stop responding to people in the workplace from a childhood-oriented perspective, and to get rid of old defenses that don't really help in workplace settings.

Now it's time to see what lurks behind those defenses.

## Befriending Your Bruises

Only you know what you've really been through in your life. No one else has the right to judge how you feel about whatever you've experienced. Though we have to *behave* according to certain cultural and legal standards as adults, there is no prescription for what we're supposed to *feel*. So it's critically important that you don't condemn yourself for your own emotions. Instead, you need to treat yourself with compassion and empathy in order to achieve the ultimate happiness and fulfillment you desire.

As I mentioned earlier, none of this means you have to go on your own personal witch-hunt, or even confront anyone from your past. In fact, you don't need anyone other than yourself in order to befriend your emotional bruises, by which I simply mean to embrace your pain and accept it for what it is, and to let go of any shame or denial about your reality. Just let it be.

Of course, as I've tried to stress throughout this book, if you've endured tremendous abuse or neglect in your life, you will need to do far more than the basic exercises I've provided below. Professional help is probably your best recourse. But don't despair. There are countless resources, whether self-help or professional, to guide your recovery from a toxic childhood. So if these suggestions only scratch the surface, take further action. Go after the forms of repair that you need. But do try the following as well.

### ▶ Compassion Exercise

I can't tell you how many people I meet who are great at being loving and understanding toward others, but who truly stink at being genuinely nice to themselves. If you're one of these people, then it's time to change. In order to befriend your pain, you have to invite it into your conscious mind and treat it with care and respect.

Spend at least fifteen minutes every day engaged in an activity that makes you feel nurtured. This doesn't have to be complicated or expensive, but you must do something. I'm sure this isn't earth-shattering news and most likely you've heard or read something like this before. But you'd be surprised how often people dismiss the simplest and easiest of helpful suggestions.

In practicing self-care, I recommend that you focus on activities that really fill your emotional holes—try to give to yourself the kinds of things of which you feel most deprived. For instance, Trina, a very charming but not very happy young woman, never had her sensual energy fostered in childhood. Early on Trina had expressed a love for nature and all living things. She could sit for hours petting a kitty or gathering and sniffing wildflowers.

Unfortunately for Trina, her parents (who were rather uptight, unemotional types) weren't very accepting of their daughter's interests. In fact, they teased her and made her feel foolish for engaging in such "unproductive nonsense." Thus, Trina grew up disregarding her sensual energies. As a result, she never felt very satisfied in life, and she continually sought dead-end jobs that never tapped into her true essence and talents. To help her find her true path, Trina started by making a bunch of arts and crafts that appealed to a variety of her senses. She used feathers, perfumes, and soft cloths. She lit candles, savored small bites of chocolate, and played the music she enjoyed.

Like Trina, you too can rediscover your buried essence by exploring various activities. Below is a list of suggestions, but please be creative and modify them according to your own needs.

- Practice meditation or yoga. (Don't worry, you don't have to stand on your head and become a pretzel. Even if you just attempt the breathing techniques of yoga, you'll be doing something soothing.)
- Use your hands creatively—knitting, pottery-making, painting, cooking, home repairs, gardening, sewing. Whatever the activity, indulge in it fully!
- Massage your own body with lotions and oils.
- Light candles and read aloud a list of positive affirmations.
- Play a sport, walk, or engage in some other form of exercise (assuming this is okay for you medically).
- Take a luxurious bath with tons of bubbles.
- Play music and sing/dance to your heart's content, or learn how to play a musical instrument.
- Write poetry. Who cares if anyone else ever reads it? Remember, this is just to get *your* emotional juices flowing.
- Rest without noises or interruptions. Turn off the phone and get some earplugs.
- Pet an animal and imagine that you're basking in the same affection.
- Watch a video or thumb through old photographs that trigger joyful memories.
- Take up a hobby.

You can certainly extend the time beyond fifteen minutes as long as the activity doesn't become a strategy to avoid other important aspects of your life. Sometimes people err on the opposite end by becoming engulfed in their own thing at the exclusion of taking care of business. It feels so good to finally be self-indulgent without guilt. But as always, it's important to strike a balance.

By carving out time each day to give yourself a gift of self-care, you are making a statement that you are important. In doing so, you are also healing old stuff. Be patient, however; this process takes time.

### ▶ Identifying Exercise

Make a list of your emotional bruises. Reflect back on the events that caused these hurts, focusing not only on the experiences themselves, but also on the consequences to your self-worth. For instance, Tessa's father often yelled at her for no particular reason. He was just chronically unhappy, and he took it out on her. For Tessa, the impact was such that she felt like she couldn't do anything right, and she never received the kind of loving contact she wanted from her dad. She felt great sadness about this loss. She also suffered anxiety, a result of fearing not only her father's wrath but also that of any male authority figure. As an adult, Tessa automatically took responsibility for things she had nothing to do with because she was so used to being irrationally blamed for things by her dad.

As you recall such instances from your childhood, make sure you keep your compassion meter revved up on high. Please note: I don't mean that you should pity yourself or feel like a victim. You're an adult now, and these old events aren't happening in the present. Even if you are currently being mistreated, then you're still in a different, far more empowered position because as an adult you have choices and options that you didn't have as a child. Pity keeps us stuck in a victim mentality, whereas compassion and appreciation allow us to breathe and grow.

As you go through this exercise, try to picture yourself as a loving parent who needs to soothe a hurt child. If you can't muster up a positive image in your own mind, then consider using a friend or relative you admire as a positive role model to emulate. If you don't have any such role models, then try going to the park and watch a nurturing and loving parent deal with her child. If you can't find any parent-image you admire, then try to recall a story or fairy tale of a nurturing parent-figure.

If you find yourself feeling bad or ashamed about what you're recollecting, verbalize something encouraging and comforting to yourself, such as, "It's okay—you're okay now. I'll protect you and keep you from harm." Or, "All of that happened in the past, I will take better care of you now." Or, "These things that hurt you also made you the person that you are, and it's my job to value you and take good care of your well-being."

The better you can "parent" yourself now, as an adult, the less you will continue to feel hurt by what you didn't get as a child. This will make it easier to keep from behaving childishly by turning your boss or coworker into the players from your youth—mom, dad, brother, sister, teacher, whomever.

### ▶ Appreciation Exercise

Over the years you may have heard one variation or another of the philosopher Friedrich Nietzsche's famous line, "What does not destroy me makes me stronger." I think it's a good thought to use as a guiding principle. You have been strengthened by whatever adversity you've endured, and this fact needs to be appreciated.

It may be hard to believe that your pain can be your best resource for learning how to thrive. But it's true. So, take a moment and give yourself a big hug. Look in the mirror and tell yourself that you are awesome for getting to where you are today. I know there are things you aren't proud of, and things you might even be holding against yourself. But try to push away those negative voices. Whatever you've been through needs to be cherished so that you can begin transforming your suffering into a resource.

Think of it this way. If you were in a disaster right now, who would you want on your side—someone who's lived a sheltered life, who's never had to deal with hardship of any sort, or someone who's walked through a desert with a broken leg and has lived to tell the story? I don't know about you, but I would vote for the one who made it through the desert. I know she'll come through in a crisis. Now, if she's also the sort of person who can tell her story with pride and humor, I'm really going to get her on my team. The message here is that whenever we've made it through adversity and we survived to tell about it, we're richer and more seasoned for the experience. When we make peace with that adversity, we have the freedom to draw upon what we've learned from it when needed.

### ▸ Commitment Exercise

It's one thing to go through the motions of being nice to yourself; it's another to allow that kindness to really sink in and to embrace the notion that self-care is a lifelong commitment. You must really put into practice the concept that it's no one else's responsibility to make your life better but your own. I hope you trust by now that I don't say this to be harsh or cruel. It's simply a reality we all must face. And once we embrace this wholeheartedly, our lives actually become less disappointing and far more manageable.

To help you cement your commitment to self-care, say the following words like a mantra when you wake up in the morning, on your drive to and from work, and just before you go to bed at night: "I'm important and deserve to be treated with respect and kindness. I'm in charge of giving this to myself, and I will continue to strive to surround myself with others who also treat me well. When I'm in situations where I feel mistreated, I will make choices that put me in a safe place, while at the same time I'll examine my own part in encouraging the mistreatment."

Of course, you don't have to say this exactly as I've written it. But whatever you choose to say, keep in mind the following three guiding principles:

1. You are in charge of your own well-being.
2. It takes two to tango in any relationship—very rarely is any one person entirely at fault for the demise of an interaction. Always be willing to accept your role in creating the drama, regardless of how small.
3. You can only control *your* own actions, reactions, and feelings, not anyone else's—so focus your attention on yourself, where you have that control.

If you have trouble committing to self-care, putting it into practice, or letting go of old hurts, please expand your resources by getting more help. You may seek other forms of self-help, focusing more specifically on your particular issues. Or you may need to seek professional counseling, especially if you've experienced serious trauma, such as being molested or abused as a child. There's nothing to be ashamed of. Remember, befriending our bruises is a critical first step in being able to have positive relationships in our personal and professional lives.

▶ *Five*

STEP TWO—
# Identify How You Make a Mess of Your Professional Life

As you proceed through this book, you'll see that I will continue to emphasize the importance of befriending your bruises and being compassionate toward yourself, and I will continue to remind you to *practice* ongoing self-care. I hope that as a result, you'll notice that you're transforming any lurking shame (the bad kind, that is) into increased self-awareness, and that you begin recognizing the importance of looking inward for the solutions to your difficulties in your workplace.

While good self-care is of the utmost importance, so too is accountability for your life in the present. In order to identify how you make a mess of your professional life, you must take a good, hard look at *your* contribution to the drama in your workplace relationships, while simultaneously maintaining self-acceptance and self-love.

Don't worry. This isn't as hard as it may sound as long as you refrain from beating yourself up. So get rid of any harsh self-criticisms and keep an open mind to self-discovery. Plus, always keep your sense of humor alert and attuned. I've noticed time and time again that the more we can be amused by our own behavior, the better chance we have of being willing and able to change that behavior should we discover that it doesn't promote our well-being.

Of course, difficult people definitely do exist in virtually every workplace. Therefore, I'm in no way suggesting that you are solely responsible for the problems you've experienced. In fact, even when you take full responsibility for whatever old stuff you've been bringing to work, you'll still discover that you simply won't be able to tolerate certain people. The fact is that some people behave very badly. It wouldn't matter how healthy you are—these people wreak havoc wherever they go. But this doesn't excuse you from trying to eliminate *your* role in these difficulties, no matter how small. In later chapters, I'll show you how to discriminate between problems that might be a reflection of your stuff and problems that result from truly offensive behavior in others. I'll also discuss tools for how to manage your interactions with these individuals. But for now, let's stay focused on what's within your own control to change—*your* behavior and how it gets you into trouble.

## What Creates Drama

I hope you've learned by this point of the book that when we've been deprived, for whatever reason, of our developmental needs, we end up with unrealistic expectations of how others should behave or treat us. And these unrealistic expectations will, inevitably, come into play at some point or another in the workplace, most often without our realizing it. We'll expect people to make up for whatever we didn't get, and we'll feel an extra dose of entitlement to behave in childlike ways should our needs continue to go unmet. Sometimes these behaviors overtly sabotage our goals. Sometimes we're not even aware that we're setting ourselves up for dysfunctional interactions with others. But whether we are conscious or unconscious of them, once these behaviors are set in motion, we won't escape their consequences.

Some of these behaviors might at first glance be viewed as positives in the workplace—for instance, doing more than your fair share of the workload. Most people would probably consider this kind of overachieving as something to strive for, rather than something that can cause problems in the workplace. So you might be thinking, "What's negative about this?" While the consequences may not be obviously negative, upon closer examination you might conclude that this behavior can pose all kinds of problems with coworkers. For instance, trying to do too much of your organization's work can lead to resentments (both within yourself and toward you from others), or it could lead to people developing unrealistic expectations of your performance. In essence, you raise the bar so high that you can't continue leaping over it month after month.

Patsi was her boss's dream employee. She would always go the extra mile on the job, never expecting additional compensation such as time off or a bonus. One day, after years of overworking, she snapped without warning. She went completely ballistic on her boss when he asked her to take work with her while she went on her yearly vacation with her family. She hadn't realized that her tendency to give so much to her job had become such an automatic reflex that she wasn't at all aware of the resentment she'd been storing. She also wasn't aware that she was ultimately responsible for having set up her boss's expectation that she'd never say no to him.

Patsi ended up in this position because she didn't want to risk being seen as a troublemaker, and she couldn't stand the thought of being disliked. Patsi never complained about being exploited because her unhealed hurts had left her with a desperate need to have everyone think well of her. She feared that any complaining would put her at risk for losing this much-needed status. She was so fearful of confrontation, and of losing others' good opinion of her, that she couldn't set healthy boundaries.

Patsi, like many of the other people whose stories I've outlined, had never received approval from her mom, though she had always been an honor student and a really good kid. After years of compensating for the absence of approval by overworking herself, she finally couldn't take it anymore. While Patsi would have initially argued that her overachievement was a positive quality, she quickly realized that this was seriously decreasing her potential for job satisfaction.

Of course, Patsi's boss had his own issues as to why he would allow Patsi to do all this extra work without compensation. This was inappropriate on his part. But Patsi didn't have control over what her boss did—she could only control herself. So it was up to her to identify and take command of her own behavior.

Because a behavior can have both positive *and* negative aspects, depending upon the context, it's best not to judge or label a particular behavior as either "good" or "bad." The real issue needs to be whether it helps you thrive. More specifically, does it help you promote positive workplace relationships? If the answer is "no," then you might consider changing behaviors, or developing new, complementary behaviors that may work better under your current circumstances. By reexamining the usefulness of a behavior and modifying it, if necessary, you empower yourself with your ability to *choose*, as opposed to being driven solely by responses that you learned in childhood to fend off painful emotions.

Below, I've tried to outline a broad spectrum of behaviors, attitudes, and beliefs that contribute to creating drama in the workplace, but this list is hardly exhaustive. Because people are so highly creative when it comes to coping, and I haven't been exposed to every possible behavior, I've come to accept that my list will never be fully comprehensive. So, if you have spotted another relevant kind of behavior, either in yourself or a coworker, that I've failed to include, feel free add it to the list. (And, if you're so inclined, please send me a note about it, and I'll add it to this list for future editions of this book.)

As you review the items below, keep a piece of paper handy. Write down the ones that you recognize in yourself. Then put a star or two next to those that really stand out in terms of how you behave. I strongly encourage you to do this exercise in writing as it will more fully highlight the information and make it more accessible. Carry your list with you as a reminder of what you're working on changing. Remember, we're prone to using our defenses whenever we feel emotionally or physically threatened, but we can minimize these when we can see clearly that we have other options.

By practicing these awareness tools, you will decrease any emerging shame and further open the door to curiosity and self-discovery. Following the list, I've included descriptions of possible consequences of these behaviors with some real-life examples of how they play out. As you read the examples, try to think of relevant scenarios from your own life. You may be tempted to make excuses for your behavior or to hide behind a defense. If so, be aware and resist the impulse. You won't be able to honestly assess your behavior if you go into a shame-hole. Remember, no one else needs to be privy to your list. You just need to be accountable to yourself. You'll be much better off once you take full ownership for your reactions and avoid placing blame on someone else. Later, you'll learn that you have many different choices for how to handle people who tend to push everyone's buttons. And by then you should also have fewer buttons to push!

### ▶ Problem Behaviors: A Review

1. Arriving late to work or leaving before you're supposed to.
2. Allowing others to do tasks originally assigned to you.
3. Ignoring instructions from your boss.
4. Performing below expectations.
5. Gossiping about others.
6. Developing inappropriate relationships with coworkers or bosses and then expecting them to grant you special favors.
7. Using company time for personal business.
8. Behaving as though you are higher ranked in the company than you truly are.
9. Acting like a know-it-all.
10. Taking credit for other people's ideas.
11. Blowing up a problem to crisis magnitude, solving it, and then wanting credit for being a hero, when in fact the problem really wasn't that big of a deal in the first place.
12. Exaggerating personal issues or problems in order to enlist sympathy from coworkers and/or to avoid workplace responsibilities.
13. Being argumentative.
14. Overachieving for the sake of getting approval from others in order to fill up holes in your self-esteem.
15. Continually working overtime without compensation.

16. Setting other people up to fail.
17. Becoming defensive when a supervisor points out a legitimate complaint concerning your behavior or job performance.
18. Dressing provocatively to get attention.
19. Making sexual gestures toward others.
20. Ignoring inappropriate behavior from others to avoid "making waves."
21. Constantly focusing on or pointing out flaws in other people's behavior.
22. Giving expensive gifts to coworkers or bosses to buy their favor.

**Arriving Late or Leaving Early.** Obviously, sometimes our lives become unmanageable—we find ourselves in an unexpected traffic jam, in the midst of a natural disaster, or we get struck with the flu. These occasional upsets are rarely the result of old bruises. But when we repeatedly shorten our workday and we're not on a flextime schedule, we're most likely acting out some unfinished business. And our coworkers won't be happy with us if we continue this behavior.

Stacy frequently came to work late. There was no doubt that she truly did have a long commute through heavy traffic. However, the problem was that Stacy allowed herself to be a victim to traffic, which was consistent and predictable, by not leaving her house earlier. Plus, she constantly distracted herself in the mornings with tasks she could have done more conveniently the night before— like doing the laundry and making her lunch. She was pointing the finger at traffic as a way to explain her behavior when, in fact, she should have been looking for the explanation from within.

Stacy hadn't been given her fair share of positive attention as a child. As a result, she had developed an unconscious belief that she didn't have to comply with rules and structure like everyone else. She wasn't malicious or consciously trying to get away with anything. In fact, she really believed that her tardiness was caused by factors outside her control. But claiming traffic as the cause of her frequent lateness kept her from being able to claim responsibility for her choices and actions. Needless to say, other people in her workplace were annoyed at her because they couldn't count on her to pull her weight when she was needed. By staying stuck in a victim mentality, she was damaging her relationships with her coworkers.

**Allowing Others to Do Your Tasks.** Every once in a while, our plates get too full and we could benefit from a little help to fulfill our job requirements. However, while it's appropriate for you to take productive steps to remedy the situation when you're overwhelmed, it's not okay to repeatedly pass assignments off onto others. If you're prone to this behavior, you're likely to create resentment in others and possibly get yourself fired.

**Ignoring Instructions from the Boss.** Oftentimes, if we have old bruises that left us fearful of confrontation, we're underequipped with the means to be assertive, and we're likely to express our aggression in passive ways. Rather than directly telling your boss that you can't do a certain task or that you don't see the value in it, you might be tempted to pretend the request doesn't exist. This kind of selective attention is bound to piss off the boss and keep you stuck in a self-defeating pattern of poor communication. This behavior may provide some excellent survival value if you're in a relationship with an irrational, abusive person, but in any other kind of situation it's like shooting yourself in the foot.

Kathleen was raised by a tyrannical single mom who treated her very badly. Kathleen survived her childhood by learning to agree with whatever her mom would say, and then simply doing whatever she wanted when her mom wasn't around. As long as she didn't get caught breaking the rules, her mom would be fairly calm. Unfortunately, Kathleen never grew to appreciate the value of structure and she had great difficulty dealing with authority figures. In the workplace, whenever she behaved as she had learned how to behave in childhood, she didn't get very far. She had to discover how to face her demons head on and learn more effective means of communicating.

**Performing Below Expectations.** Sometimes we encounter people in the workplace who can never be satisfied, no matter how exceptional our performance. In these cases, it's futile to try to excel. But for many people, underperformance stems from childhood experiences where they learned that they could never please their caregivers. They've then transferred these feelings into their work lives, where they're unable to give a decent effort. These individuals often lack feelings of positive self-regard, or have an irrational fear of either failure or success.

Craig, a truly brilliant engineer, wasn't living up to his professional potential. He was too afraid to outshine his coworkers for fear of their envy or jealousy. Unfortunately, Craig had learned to downplay his intelligence because his dad, Jim, couldn't tolerate having a son who appeared smarter than he. Craig carried this old bruise into the workplace by doing mediocre work, often making careless mistakes. His boss couldn't understand why Craig turned in such sloppy work, because Craig had scored very high on performance tests he'd been given when he applied for the job. Good news for Craig, though. Once he figured out the connection between his childhood bruise and his job performance, he was able to start producing to his full potential.

**Gossiping.** Let's face it. We're all tempted to dig up a little dirt on other people and spread the word about their flaws. It's human nature to sometimes put other people down in order to make our own selves feel better. Just look at how popular tabloid news has become. But while this might seem like harmless fun, it can lead to severe consequences in the workplace. Whether you're the instigator of gossip, or someone who just passively listens, you become a player in creating drama.

Keep in mind that gossiping is not the same as making a legitimate complaint to the appropriate people when someone you work with behaves out of line. In these situations, it's important to take action to help remedy the problem. What's inappropriate is talking about people behind their backs, whether the information you're transmitting is true or false. If you're prone to gossiping, do your best to stay conscious of this tendency and then refrain whenever you spot yourself slipping up. Take action to become busier and more challenged at work to reduce the allure of gabbing about others. Even if you engage a little but manage to pull yourself out quickly, you're demonstrating progress. And try to figure out what you get out of gossiping by using hurts from childhood as the framework for your answer. Save your gossip impulse for the chitter-chatter you have with your friends about your favorite film and TV stars.

**Developing Inappropriate Relationships and Expecting Special Favors.** Judy had a special knack for schmoozing with her coworkers, especially with her boss. She was a master at getting people to appreciate her charming and lively personality. But Judy wasn't all peaches and cream. Judy manipulated people into adoring her, although she didn't do this consciously or maliciously. Then she would take advantage of those who became close to her by constantly asking them for favors.

Not long after befriending a coworker, she would ask for things like to get lunch for her, pick up her laundry, and pass along memos that were her responsibility to deliver. One might feel sorry for Judy, knowing that she had been treated harshly by her father. He had been much harder on her than he had been on her other siblings, making her do extra chores, relentlessly pushing her to excel in school, and forcing her to act more mature than her peers. He didn't want to harm her. In fact, he thought she was more "special" than the others, and believed she was the child who had the most potential to succeed. Nevertheless, Judy felt seriously taken advantage of and felt deprived of having fun as a kid. In her mind, as an adult, it seemed only fair that others should lighten her load. But, even though no one would argue that Judy had not had it rough, she didn't have a right to make others pay for how she had been wronged. And her carrying on this way with her peers ultimately kept her trapped by her old stuff. Eventually others felt they were being manipulated.

This form of coping commonly results from all sorts of emotional bruising. But doing this in the workplace will prevent you from establishing healthy relationships and keeps you from being responsible for yourself.

**Using Company Time for Personal Business.** People use work hours to do all kinds of inappropriate personal business. People surf the internet, make dinner reservations, pay bills, telephone friends, and so on, all while on company time rather than on their breaks. Some even go so far as to manage a secondary business at their company's expense. If your coworkers see you do these things and they don't take the same liberties, they're likely to resent you. This tends to be the case even if you've been given permission. And, as I've repeatedly pointed out, resentment leads to drama.

There are all sorts of reasons why people feel entitled to use company time take care of personal matters—boredom, procrastination, not having enough work, or feeling like there isn't enough time in the day to get everything else done. On the surface, these all seem legitimate. But I think the better explanation is that when people misuse company time, it's because (on some level) they believe they shouldn't have to abide by the rules. In the end, whatever the reasons, behaving this way devalues the importance of our work and alienates others who respect the workplace structure.

Of course, conducting personal business during legitimate breaks like your lunch hour doesn't violate professional codes and shouldn't pose a problem. In these cases, if someone resents you, then you can rest assured that it's not your issue, but theirs.

**Behaving as Though Higher-Ranked.** If we didn't receive enough positive strokes to our egos as kids, we may compensate by acting like we think we're superior. We don't act this way to put others down, so much, but more to stave off our own underlying feelings of inferiority or inadequacy. In the workplace, this commonly shows up as behaving as if you're irreplaceable. This tends to make other people angry or hurt because they will likely perceive that you are looking down on them. Or they'll just think that you are a jerk and then won't want to have much to do with you.

**Acting Like a Know-It-All.** This is similar to upping your rank, but it's more pervasive. Know-it-alls have great difficulty being able to admit mistakes or acknowledge ignorance in any given area. Of course, the reality is that no one can ever know everything about everything. If your childhood background left you fearful of appearing stupid, then it can be very, very tough to acknowledge things that you don't know or understand. But most people don't trust know-it-alls. Behaving this way is likely to result in exactly what you fear—people are going to think you're foolish.

**Taking Credit for Other People's Ideas.** This can be especially tempting if you work with someone who gets a disproportionate amount of the glory despite not being a star performer. If you have any unfinished sibling rivalry, you might be particularly prone to this behavior.

Cassie worked for a large corporation. Within her department, one of her coworkers, Jill, seemed to get far more of the accolades and attention from their boss than the rest of the employees. Most everyone resigned themselves to this obvious favoritism—Jill was a bombshell, and the boss, who was clearly smitten with her, gave her special attention as a result. (Certainly not appropriate behavior on the part of the boss—but the reality nonetheless.)

Cassie, who had always taken a back seat to her beautiful older sister, was completely thrown off by this inequity. Cassie, of course, had blocked her childhood hurt from conscious memory. She had many professional strengths of her own, but she was so desperate to get the kind of recognition from the boss that Jill received that she even resorted to taking credit for other people's ideas in an effort to win the boss's favor. She couldn't accept that this was a lost cause. Her boss would never be able to respect and appreciate anyone's good work. Cassie was wasting her time. But until Cassie healed this old bruise, she behaved in ways that caused her to lose her coworkers' respect.

**Blowing Up a Problem to Get Greater Credit for Solving It.** I think there's a bit of drama queen in all of us. But whether or not we make this our primary style of interacting with others has a lot to do with our childhood bruises. If we didn't get the positive attention necessary to build healthy self-esteem, we might develop a tendency to embellish or exaggerate a problem so that we can reap a higher reward for solving it.

Tonya's brother was the star in their family. He was great at sports, got good grades at school, and was very popular among his peers. Tonya, on the other hand, kept more to herself because she felt shy and awkward around other people. She was a pretty good student but didn't make friends easily. Her mom, the family's primary caregiver, almost ignored Tonya while totally indulging her brother. Tonya figured out early on that she would get noticed only when she created a crisis. For instance, when she would fall off her bike and skin her knee, she would exaggerate the pain and plead for tender loving care. This seemed to be the only way to get her mom's attention.

At Tonya's job in a retail clothing store, she would report the details of each day to her boss, underlining even the most mundane things with great intensity. By the end of her description, one would think that she'd rescued whole communities of victims from a hurricane. Sometimes her coworkers would be amused, but other times they would get fed up with Tonya's need to exaggerate the trivial.

**Exaggerating Personal Issues.** Sometimes we feel so burdened and out of control in our personal lives that we don't have the energy required to do our jobs well. In the best scenario, we recognize our limitations and negotiate with our boss for extra time off or for flex-time hours so we can address our important personal obligations outside of the workplace—like a new baby, a divorce, or a sick parent who needs our care. However, many people don't know how to approach their superiors in a mature, responsible way. These people often don't feel entitled to consider anything other than work to be important. Their self-esteem depends on their job performance. Or they feel too much entitlement, to the point where they don't believe that they should have to keep their personal stuff outside of the workplace exactly *because* their lives are so out of control. Hence, they feel like victims and expect people in the workplace to function as their psychotherapists or surrogate parents. This dynamic is especially common for people who have endured childhood abuse.

Jasmine grew up in a home environment filled with conflict, chaos, and even violence. For Jasmine, life truly was a 24/7 crisis. Because Jasmine received so few tools to help her have successful relationships in adulthood, her life was in constant turmoil. Eventually, though, she discovered that *she* generated a big chunk of the drama in her life. She also learned that some of the things that she always thought were a big deal really weren't anything to sweat about after all. Nevertheless, she continually re-created the drama from her childhood in her adult life, professionally and personally. For a while, her coworkers were sympathetic, but soon they would tire of her excuses as to why she couldn't do her fair share of work.

**Being Argumentative.** Many of us like a good debate now and again, but if we *always* need to drive our point home, we can really be annoying to others. Many people (though not all) who have grown up in high-conflict families feel most comfortable and familiar with dispute and confrontation. They may have trouble going with the flow, and conditions of peace and tranquility just don't feel normal to them.

There's nothing wrong with pursuing a point if it's truly meaningful and important. What doesn't work so well is arguing for the sake of arguing. Many people get really turned off to people who seem driven to create disagreement. Many who are prone to arguing may actually claim to dislike it, yet they seem compelled to conflict despite consciously wishing for more peace. If you find yourself embroiled in constant arguments, pay close attention to how much you are actually the one setting up this dynamic with others, and work hard to back away when you feel the argumentative bug taking over in your dealings with others. As I counsel parents of teenagers, always be very careful to pick and choose your battles. This is also a good general rule in the workplace.

**Overachieving for Approval.** I don't know too many bosses who would turn away a perfectionist who constantly exceeds expectations. However, as a recovering perfectionist myself, I can tell you that this kind of behavior comes with a very high price.

Superachievers eventually burn out. And more often than not, their excessive efforts go unappreciated by those the overachiever aims to please. Remember Darcy and Patsi? No matter what they did, they didn't get the accolades they so deeply desired. Also, superachievers believe they are encouraging feelings of fondness from coworkers, when in fact they're often perceived as unapproachable and even arrogant. In the end, there is no boost in self-esteem. Everyone loses.

**Continually Working Overtime Without Compensation.** This is a subset of the above. People who work overtime without compensation tend to pass on taking their breaks, skip lunch, come into work earlier than their peers, and leave much later. They think they're demonstrating incredible commitment and dedication. And sometimes these qualities are necessary, depending on one's specific job and career goals. However, if this kind of behavior is motivated more by a fear of losing others' approval, or by a lack of self-respect, all that extra work will most likely become a problem. You'll end up being exploited by others, and you won't be taken seriously once you do express your limits.

**Seeking Approval to Bolster Self-Esteem.** We all crave recognition and acknowledgment for a job well done. And we might even modify our general demeanor a bit in order to get these rewards. For instance, we might put on a happy face even when we feel grumpy, or we might compliment a coworker's outfit even when we're really not that fond of it. Most of these gestures help make for a more pleasant workplace environment. However, when we go overboard—think "sucking up"—we're likely to make more enemies than friends among our coworkers. And any astute boss will likely see the disingenuousness of this behavior.

To create positive relationships, we first need to feel good about ourselves from the inside. The recognition we get from others should be a bonus, not what we count on for sustenance. Coworkers and bosses can't make up for what we didn't get from our caregivers. We have to take responsibility for learning how to get these good feelings and affirmations from ourselves (through good self-care) and from those people in our inner circle of friends and loved ones.

**Setting People Up to Fail.** Sometimes we secretly hope that a coworker will fail so that we look better in the eyes of our supervisors and peers. Usually we're not even conscious of this tendency. Granted, if you were on a deserted island with only a limited supply of food, your life-affirming instinct to get your share of the food (and some to spare) would serve you well. If your childhood experiences were such that you could only get love and attention at the expense of someone else, then you're going to be prone to seeing all situations as a fight for survival. This means you might unknowingly set up competitions between yourself and others. But while the workplace can at times be a cutthroat place, very rarely is it ever necessary to sabotage someone else in order to climb the ladder yourself. Focusing on being your own shining star will usually suffice.

**Becoming Defensive.** As already noted in the previous chapter, most of us have developed defense mechanisms we draw upon under conditions of physical or emotional danger. These have great survival value, but they won't help you thrive. True, some people in the workplace will be always be hypercritical, in ways that range from unconstructive to outright destructive. However, the reality is that in the workplace, it's perfectly appropriate for people to give us honest feedback, and we need to have the inner strength to be able to respond to this feedback with willing openness. That doesn't mean that we have to digest everything dished out to us without question. But we do need to create emotional boundaries flexible enough to at least listen and take into account the feedback we're offered. This becomes much easier when we have learned to accept both our real strengths and our real limitations.

Tara was teased and put down by her older brother. Her parents, usually exasperated by their children's constant bickering, often failed to intervene in ways that would have prevented some of the insecurities Tara later developed. As a way of protecting herself as best she could, the young Tara stuck by the saying, "Sticks and stones could break my bones, but words can never hurt me." The truth, however, was that Tara was terribly hurt by her brother's insults.

However, to keep from feeling the intensity of that hurt, Tara became very defensive and resistant anytime anyone had anything even slightly negative to point out to her. This put her at quite a disadvantage in her workplace, because any mistakes in her highly specialized job could seriously cost the company. She needed to learn how to be more receptive to having her work scrutinized and not take acknowledgment of her mistakes as signs of personal failure. Luckily for Tara, she was able to make the connection between her past experiences and her present behavior. Making this link enabled her to see that the methods of protection she learned in childhood were harming her in the workplace. She accepted that her superiors had a right to be critical (as long as they weren't coming across as malicious or humiliating) and that she could handle the feedback. And, sometimes when their input seemed inaccurate, she learned how to apply different, more effective means of disagreeing without putting up her porcupine quills.

**Dressing Provocatively.** Now, I understand this is a very subjective judgment. What might be considered acceptable attire in one environment could be construed as quite inappropriate in another. For instance, if you're going out dancing with your friends and a miniskirt with a midriff top keeps you stylin'—well, if someone else has an issue with your outfit, that's her problem. (Though I think it's always best to understand that the clothes we wear invite certain reactions, and we need either to be okay with those reactions or to make different choices.) Then again, if you're taking clients out on a company lunch and you're sexing it up to get more attention, this can pose quite a problem. People who tend to feel insecure or who were inappropriately sexualized as children often have difficulty assessing the impact of the clothes they wear.

Brittany, a thirty-five-year-old pharmaceutical representative, loved the attention she received for her great legs. She had been one of those girls who everyone loved to hate because she got lots of attention for her appearance in her teen years. Brittany had never received much respect for her other attributes, like her intelligence and kindness. Unfortunately, her self-worth became based largely on being a hottie.

As a result, in the workplace Brittany wore skirts far too short and blouses far too low-cut. Sure, lots of men she encountered were turned on by how she dressed and flirted with her. Brittany found this kind of behavior comfortable and familiar. But as time went on, she grew increasingly resentful that her appearance was the only thing about her that ever got noticed. She learned that by changing her look, she would lose some of this attention—but she also paved the way for commanding more respect and appreciation for her sales skills.

**Making Sexual Gestures.** Being friendly, playful, and complimentary toward others can increase morale and positive energy in the workplace. Though friendliness can sometimes be seen as flirting, this doesn't have to be a problem as long as it's left at this amicable level and doesn't involve any suggestive sexual connotations. However, anything beyond that enters the murky realm of covert or overt sexual harassment.

People who've been objectified and sexualized during their childhoods are more likely to end up in situations where they're revictimized in this manner. The flip side of this is that they might identify with the people who afflicted them this way, coping by treating it as no big deal, and then growing up to treat other people in a similarly demeaning fashion. This kind of behavior simply can't be part of the workplace environment. If it were up to me, all companies would have a zero-tolerance policy for unwanted sexual advances.

Does this mean that people can never hook up romantically in the workplace? Not necessarily—but the boundaries have to be *very* clearly defined and thoroughly acceptable to all of the people involved. Later on in this book I'll delve deeper into office romance and its potential consequences. But for now, suffice it to say that if your communications with coworkers feature sexual undertones, you need to take a very serious look at this behavior. The consequences can be far more severe than losing your job. Or if you've been the victim of sexual harassment, you need to learn more about how to head this behavior off at the pass. (See Chapter Nine for more on this topic.)

**Ignoring Inappropriate Behavior to Avoid "Making Waves."** Sometimes it makes sense to not make a big deal out of someone else's inappropriate behavior, depending upon the seriousness of the offense. For instance, a coworker has taken extra-long lunch breaks for the past two weeks, and you need her presence in order to complete a task. Should you confront the coworker about it, or even take the issue to your boss? A case can certainly be made for either "yes" or "no." But you would need to gather more information to make an informed decision. More importantly, you need to be alert to whether you are making a conscious choice to let something go (after having fully evaluated the pros and cons of pointing it out), or whether you're reflexively avoiding confrontation because of old stuff causing you to be fearful. The criterion in these cases should be whether addressing the behavior would actually benefit the workplace experience. And if the answer is "yes," then you need to learn how to proceed assertively.

**Focusing on Flaws in Other People's Behavior.** This is the flip side to ignoring behavior to avoid making waves, but it can be equally disruptive to your workplace experience. Someone who continually points out small misbehaviors among his or her coworkers will appear to others to be a tattletale. And we all know how annoying a tattletale can be. However, that doesn't mean that we should never open our mouths when we see an injustice, inequity, or violation. But always make sure that you've cleaned up your side of the street before you start pointing fingers at anyone else's messes.

**Giving Expensive Gifts.** Of course, this is another relative judgment. I once had a patient who gave me a very expensive gift, though it cost her nothing (a perk of her job), and even if she had paid for it, it would have been insignificant in comparison to what most other folk could afford since she earned what most of us would consider a very hefty salary. Thus, I had to refrain from my usual response to better understand the meaning behind the gift. That is, sometimes patients will give their therapists expensive gifts because deep down inside they feel as though they are not very important. In this case, my patient was just making a grateful gesture.

The above example, however, isn't always what's really going on. Some people do believe that their value is based on how much they can give materially to another. But there can be many consequences to this behavior in the workplace. For one, the person doing the giving continues to keep alive the old bruise that she is not of value to others were it not for giving out such nice gifts. This feeds her belief that her other qualities aren't important. Two, those who receive the gifts often feel uncomfortable and recognize that they're not appropriate to the relationship or circumstance. And three, other people who don't give expensive gifts might feel inadequate and then resentful or fearful that they don't provide the same.

▶ *Letting Go Exercise*

I hope the above list and accompanying illustrations have given you food for thought regarding how you create drama in the workplace. If you happen to notice that you fit many of the descriptions, don't be alarmed. No doubt we've all been guilty of at least some of these behaviors at one time or another. But now that you've identified how you mess up your professional life, you have the power to clean it up.

To help you achieve cleaner, more peaceful interactions at work, commit yourself to addressing each of the items you've checked off for at least one week. Take particular care to notice when the negative behavior or attitude shows up, and then work toward altering your behavior as quickly as possible. Challenge yourself to do the opposite of what you would typically do. For instance, if you avoid dealing with problematic behaviors in others, set a goal of taking at least one situation and approaching it head-on instead of avoiding it. If you tend to participate in water-cooler gossip, practice a tighter lip and see what happens. Or, if you tend to perform below expectations, see what it's like to go the extra mile (though not to the point of excess).

As you press yourself to try different approaches, keep in mind that habits are hard to break and we all tend to stick with what's most familiar, despite any negative consequences. But anytime you change your reaction to a situation, and practice a more proactive, constructive style, you begin to build up your repertoire of positive responses. And eventually, with practice, these new behaviors can become the norm. The ineffective behaviors will have less and less power and the more constructive approaches will eventually carry more weight. Above all, be creative. Experiment with the unknown. Make this exercise part of your daily ritual. You'll be surprised at how quickly you can start to see positive results.

# Six

STEP THREE—
# Understand Transference: Recognizing That Your Boss Is *Not* Your Mother, and Other Workplace Relationship Dilemmas

While I was formulating this book, I first thought I would put this chapter right up front because it focuses sharply on the process of how we replicate our old stuff in our adult relationships. Basically, it offers the substance behind the explanations. But I quickly reconsidered. I remembered how, when I was in graduate school, I found it so difficult to comprehend certain ideas in the abstract. So I opted to supply lots of examples first, in the earlier chapters, and *then* introduce the term here. I hope I've managed to spare you the psychobabble for as long as possible, until we've gone over enough useful illustrations to better understand the specialized terms. In essence, you've learned a recipe, you've eaten, and you've begun digesting the meal. Now I'll tell you what the dish is called. In this way, I think you'll have a better chance of remembering this concept and applying it to your relationships in the workplace.

Psychologists describe a very important concept using the term *transference*. Don't worry. You don't need an advanced degree to understand transference. And I'll try to define it as simply as possible. Though please, keep in mind that transference is one of those things that's hard to describe in few words. But, since I've already provided so many illustrations, I think you'll grasp it pretty quickly. But if you don't catch on right away, have some faith that you will as you read on.

Transference is what happens between two individuals where one person projects onto another person her feelings, thoughts, and reactions that have much more to do with an older relationship than her relationship with this other person. While these projections could come from feelings related to anyone from one's life, they usually have the most power when they've stemmed from early interactions with parents, siblings, and other important figures from our childhoods.

To help clarify, picture two circles overlapping in the center just a bit. The left circle holds old memories, experiences, and feelings. The right circle holds whatever is happening to you in the present while you're interacting with someone. Most of the time, present interactions will have some resemblance to interactions or relationships we've had with other people in our lives. However, when we blend these two circles together, with the left circle fully engulfing the right one, then we're stuck in a transference reaction. We're no longer able to see the differences between what was and what is.

Basically, the less conscious we are of our old bruises and how they affect us, the more likely we are to have transference reactions, which result in our behaving in ways that are driven by old experiences. Conversely, the more aware we become of our old stuff, the better prepared we are to keep it from affecting our current relationships. It's doubtful that anyone can ever be fully rid of transference, but we can definitely temper its influence by becoming more conscious of it.

To further illustrate this concept, let's say that you had a wrathful father who was prone to raising his voice and then, within a few moments, taking a swat at you. You were terrified of his anger, so you did the best you could to keep yourself from harm without further angering your father. Now, in the present, you have a job where you work with someone who tends to get loud and animated when he's upset, but he's not at all physically violent. But because of your experiences with your dad, you've come to associate a raised voice with violence and fear. If you respond to your coworker with the same fear and defensiveness as you did to your father when you were a child, then you're having a transference reaction. However, if you're able to recognize that this coworker's similarity to your father stops at the raising of the voice, and is therefore not threatening or harmful, then you'll be less likely to experience transference. Your responses will be generated by your current reality, rather than by your old bruises.

We all have transference reactions of one kind or another, whether we're aware of them or not. Even when we're most attuned to what is truly happening in the present, we're still prone to transference reactions during times of stress or vulnerability. However, the more we heal our old stuff, and the better we understand our tendencies toward this process, the better we'll be at nipping transference reactions in the bud before they get out of control and prompt us to behave inappropriately.

While I'm pointing out the dark side of transference, I should also point out that this process doesn't have to be negative. You can also have a positive transference toward someone. But while positive projections based on old experiences may not necessarily need to be as heavily scrutinized as negative projections, we still need to be conscious of them because they're not based on the present reality. Thus, they could backfire and get you into trouble.

When Toby was hired as an emergency room nurse, she'd been interviewed by the charge nurse, Ella, who initially struck her as having a very pleasant and soft-spoken demeanor similar to that of Toby's mom. Toby had always been very close to her mom and her childhood was filled with much love and care. Naturally, Ella's resemblance to Toby's mom was enough to set in motion a positive transference.

Based on her pleasant associations with Ella's manner, Toby let down her professional guard, believing she had nothing to be concerned about with her new boss. However, as time rolled on, Ella displayed many other far less favorable qualities. In fact, it turned out that Toby's initial impression of Ella didn't have much to do with Ella's behavior in the workplace. Beneath Ella's pleasant façade was a quick-tempered, highly demanding, and unreasonable grouch.

Initially, Toby kept her head in the sand and tried to rationalize Ella's behavior as out of character. But it was actually Ella's interviewing behavior that had been out of character. Unfortunately, Toby's positive projections kept her naïve and unprepared for what was to come. After a few weeks, Toby received a lambasting from Ella for having misfiled one of a patient's charts. Mind you, this was Toby's first offense, hardly enough to tarnish her impeccable record.

I'm not suggesting that Toby would have been better off starting out with suspicion or distrust. However, had she been more aware of the transference she was experiencing, she might have been able to stay more neutral and get to know Ella better, across many different situations and interactions, before automatically assuming positive things about her character. In doing so, she might have been better equipped to keep a closer watch and be less vulnerable to attack. Through understanding transference, Toby learned that the similarities between her mother and Ella were far fewer than their differences.

Sometimes our transference reactions prove fitting to our current situation. For example, your boss may turn out to have a very similar personality and way of responding to someone who mistreated or hurt you during your childhood. After all, nobody has a monopoly on any particular behavior or personality type. But it's good to have a lot of information first before jumping to these sorts of conclusions. The best way to deal with transference is to recognize when you're experiencing it and view it as just a sample of the information necessary to fully evaluate a person or situation in the workplace (or in any relationship) than to let it run the show.

## Sources of Transference

Transference comes in many varieties and shows no favoritism to gender, age, race, or socioeconomic status. Transference can occur in new or established relationships. It can be big or small, positive or negative. Whatever might trigger transference in one person may have the opposite effect on someone else. For instance, let's look at Trina and Helen, who both worked for the same boss, Charles, within a large mortgage company.

Charles was in charge of about fifteen people. According to Trina, he got along fine with most of his team except her. And he seemed exceptionally attentive to one other woman, Helen. Both of these women reacted very strongly to him, but in opposite ways and beyond what seemed appropriate to the situation. Trina couldn't stand him, whereas Helen thought he walked on water.

Charles reminded Trina of her father, whom she described as very arrogant and insensitive. To her, Charles seemed cold, distant, and unfriendly, and she spent a good chunk of her workday upset because she felt she couldn't please him. Helen, Trina's friend and coworker, believed that Charles acted quite professionally and that he was someone to be admired. So how could this be—two intelligent women, working for the same man, having two entirely different experiences?

Actually this isn't as weird as it sounds. Just as two adult siblings can have very different memories of what happened in their family during childhood, it's also very common for two people in the workplace to have dramatically different reactions to a coworker or boss. In the above scenario, because of Trina's emotional bruises from her childhood, she perceived her boss's behavior as far more negative than she might have had she not felt deprived of emotional nurturing. Unbeknownst to Trina, she lived in hope for a relationship with a boss that would be more akin to that between a loving parent and child. She expected Charles to make up for what she never got from her father. And because Charles wasn't the most emotionally demonstrative guy, she interpreted his manner as being cold and distant.

Helen, on the other hand, had felt smothered by her parents. They constantly meddled in her life and continually disregarded her attempts to maintain some privacy. Unlike Trina, Helen experienced Charles's neutrality and minimal display of emotion as refreshingly freeing. He gave her much-needed breathing room.

Transference can happen among people of any age, any gender, and any position in the workplace hierarchy. You can project mother stuff onto a female or male coworker, or onto your boss. Or you might transfer old father stuff onto a male or female coworker or boss. You might also have a sister or brother transference happening, or maybe something unresolved with a former teacher who influenced your development. Say you were bullied by a peer in grade school—the fear you experienced back then might be triggered by a nasty coworker. Transference can originate from interactions with earlier caregivers or from other important people from our childhood. Or it can be generated by experiences with past or current lovers or friends. You can even have a transference reaction with a child, wherein the child's behavior triggers the unconscious image of your own parent. (You might look out for this in your personal life if you have kids of your own.) Any combination is possible.

Transference doesn't imply insanity. In fact, the capacity to make assumptions about others based on automatic reactions can be a very useful mechanism to help fill in gaps when we have holes in our information.

For example, imagine you're in a business meeting and you don't have time to get to know all of the people required to attend the meeting. You have to give a presentation and you're expected to be sharp and entertaining. Yet, you have no real knowledge of the likes, dislikes, or interests of the individuals in the group. You can see that in this type of setting, it would be helpful to make some quick assessments. The only means you have for making such assessments is by drawing upon your past experiences. You simply don't have the time to get to know everyone.

Ideally however, healing your old bruises will let you draw upon the sum total of all of your experiences—not just those associated with emotional hurts. And when you become aware that you are making these projections, you'll be able to adjust if you see that they're having a negative effect. When transference takes hold of you, you lose your ability to choose. Once this happens, you're bound to resort to more childlike behavior—not pretty in the workplace.

## Transference Traps

Tons of things can trigger transference reactions. Here are just a few of the many different things that can catch you up in "transference traps":

- **Mannerisms** People convey many different emotions through their body language. Most of us have certain ways we carry ourselves and move our bodies. Depending on your personal history, the body language of a coworker or boss could trigger transference reactions.

  Tiffany's boss, June, had a very slight build. She walked stiffly with very erect posture. Before Tiffany was able to identify the triggers, this drove her nuts. Every time she had to cross paths with June, she wished she could run for the hills. Fortunately, Tiffany wasn't required to have much fact-to-face contact with her boss.

  Through some digging into her past, we learned that Tiffany's parents had used the same babysitter for several years when Tiffany was young. Though her memory was a bit vague, she recalls the sitter as having been really uptight and unreasonably strict—and with a walk very much like June's. When Tiffany had complained to her parents, they dismissed her as being "too sensitive." Tiffany had carried her frustration over this exchange around with her for years and had no idea that it could rear its head in the workplace.

- **Tone of voice** This category includes everything about one's voice, such as quality, pitch, volume, and cadence. One of Trisha's coworkers had a high-pitched voice that Trisha described as "very squeaky." It reminded Trisha very much of her sister's voice, and Trisha felt that her sister had always gotten far more attention than she had. Whenever Trisha had to interact with this coworker, she would cringe. Sure enough, because she hadn't connected the transference dots, she was reacting to this coworker as she would to her sister, ready to feel cheated out of something she thought belonged to her—like praise from their boss.

- **Smell** I don't mean that someone has to smell bad to trigger a reaction. Delia's boss wore a particular perfume that reminded her of her grandmother, whom Delia had always experienced as very obnoxious, loud, and domineering. Delia's mother never stood up to her, and Delia often felt mistreated by Granny. To make matters worse, Granny had lived in their home for a couple of years. From ages seven to ten, Delia had even shared her bed with her grandmother, which she had hated. She never forgot the smell of Granny's perfume, which permeated the room and made Delia feel nauseous. Needless to say, just the scent of Delia's coworker triggered a negative transference reaction.
- **Style of dress** Susan's employee, Carol, wore very short skirts and tight tops to the workplace that were rather inappropriate for her line of work as a bank teller. However, Susan's reaction to Carol's dress was well beyond what was appropriate, too. Susan responded to Carol's appearance with feelings of rage and inadequacy. Carol had the body type that Susan saw as the ideal—apparently, just like Susan's younger sister, Barb. As it turns out, Barb had stolen many of Carol's boyfriends during their adolescence.

  Someone's style of dress doesn't have to be inappropriate to trigger a reaction. Whether someone is fashionable or geeky, it doesn't matter. And a transference reaction might even be triggered by a specific outfit.
- **Physical characteristics** Have you ever found yourself feeling a sense of familiarity with someone you've never met because she reminds you of a close friend or relative? Have you ever been slightly repulsed or turned off by someone whom you've never met, not really understanding why? There's a good chance these reactions

were triggered by transference. Even after you get to know someone, you might be prone to transference in any given moment as people's expressions can change how they appear physically.

One woman I worked with, Sheila, had a transference reaction to her own face. As she matured, she grew to look more and more like her mother. Though Sheila indicated that her mother was quite beautiful, and no one in their right mind would complain about looking like her, this was still a nightmare for Sheila because her mother had been horribly abusive. Sheila had to find a way to disconnect her appearance from her memories of abuse. The similarities didn't have to be generalized by the pressure of transference.

- **Personality Characteristics** We all have a style with which we approach the world. Ideally, we're able to modify that style, and our behavior, according to the demands of a situation or relationship. The more flexible we are, the better chance we have of coping well with a variety of experiences. However, we all tend to have a basic temperament that makes us unique.

Some of us are more gregarious than others, some more emotional, some more thoughtful, and some more cautious. If you were raised by a mom with a bubbly personality and she treated you kindly, then you might be likely to have positive associations regarding someone in the office who's also bubbly. Or conversely, if your mom had a bubbly personality but she was also a raging nag, then you might come to associate this quality with more negative impressions.

Kelly's mom had what I call the "caffeine personality." She was always jittery, jumpy, impatient, and rather forceful in her commands. Kelly, a much more laid-back type, longed for peace and quiet. She liked hanging around with mellow people. So wouldn't you know it? She landed herself a job with a hyperactive boss who couldn't sit still. He wasn't ill-tempered in any way, but he resembled Kelly's mom in terms of his energy level. Kelly continually found herself getting worked up by her boss's anxious demeanor. However, once she made the transference connection, she was able to deal with him in a much calmer fashion.

Tony's dad, Frank, was a "blamer" who was quite proficient at the hot-potato defense. He would never take responsibility for his own behavior or mistakes. Everything that went wrong was always someone else's fault. Tony had no idea how much this had affected him growing up. He carried a lot of resentment for having been falsely accused so many times in his youth. The situation was so bad that if Frank knocked over a glass of water and Tony was anywhere within earshot, Frank would blame Tony for his own accident and make him clean it up.

While pursuing an acting career during his early twenties, Tony worked in a restaurant waiting tables. Unfortunately, Tony's manager at the restaurant, Paul, turned out to be another blamer. Just like Frank, Paul saw himself as perfect and everyone and everything else as flawed. For instance, he wouldn't schedule enough servers on a dinner shift, and the restaurant would get so packed that there would be hour-long waits for tables. Customers would complain about poor service. But rather than fess up to being understaffed (his responsibility), he would yell at the servers for being incompetent.

Of course, Tony had every reason to be annoyed at being dumped on whenever something went wrong. However, rather than recognize that this was his manager's problem, Tony personalized it and felt like a little boy once again being wrongly accused by his dad. He lost sight of his option to quit and find another job, or simply to let this obnoxious behavior of Paul's just roll off his back.

Tony wasn't projecting something that wasn't really happening—in fact, Paul really did behave just like Frank. But his situation was a transference trap nonetheless, because it led Tony to regress into childlike behavior. He wasn't able to recognize that his manager didn't really have any real power or control over him.

- **Environmental or Situational Triggers** I have a great example of this from my own life. When I was taking my oral exam for my license to practice psychology, I experienced an enormous amount of anxiety. I later realized that I wasn't so anxious because of the exam, per se, but because of the conditions under which the exam was given. The exam was being given in a hotel room with two twin beds and a little table. I was the very last candidate of the day and I was in this small room with two men. I had gone through a number of experiences in my teenage years where I'd been physically violated in environments similar to this one, and some of this old stuff became activated outside of my conscious awareness. Mind you, these examiners were quite nice, and I'm certain they were harmless. But my body was seeing a very different picture than the reality. My projections caused me this huge amount of unnecessary stress.

  Anything concerning an office's ambience or the way it's laid out can have triggering potential. The location of your work area juxtaposed to that of your boss could trigger old vulnerabilities and transference reactions. Or the ways in which the company conducts its internal meetings could serve as a trigger. The examples are endless.

▸ *Reflection Exercise*

Take a moment to reflect on the ways in which you fall victim to transference traps in your office. Jot down whatever comes to mind. Put your list aside, as later you'll expand on it.

## Countertransference

Now that you've got an understanding of transference, understanding the next big term I'm throwing at you—*countertransference*—will be a piece of cake. Essentially, countertransference (leading to the *countertransference trap*) is a reaction you have to someone else's transference. Countertransference has all the properties of transference. However, where transference can occur regardless of how someone actually behaves, countertransference comes about when you realize that stuff being projected onto you is irrational, but you still can't keep from reacting irrationally to it. Basically, you see the insanity, but you can't respond sanely because the insanity is pushing your buttons. Thus, as with transference, countertransference results in your not having control over your own responses.

As I've mentioned earlier, everyone is subject to at least the occasional transference reaction. So naturally, in the same way everyone is subject to possible countertransference traps. Typically, wherever you find transference, you'll find some countertransference lurking around.

Countertransference, like transference, is an emotional response generated because of old unhealed bruises. It shows no favoritism to rank, age, gender, race, or intelligence. Whether you have the best or the worst workplace behavior, you could be the target of someone's transference. Remember, transference can be triggered by just about anything. So at some point in time, it's quite likely that your mere presence might push someone's buttons and trigger a transference trap. If this projection in turn pushes any of your buttons, you're bound to have a countertransference reaction.

Adrianna, a supermarket manager, got along pretty well with most of her staff except for one person—Justine. Justine wasn't really sure why Adrianna had it in for her, but according to Justine, Adrianna was always snapping at her for no apparent reason. When Justine looked back on her prior work history, she couldn't recall ever having received this kind of reaction from anyone. She was really perplexed as to why she had become Adrianna's scapegoat. Over time, it became harder and harder for Justine to rationalize her boss's behavior, especially as it became more and more evident that Adrianna only acted this way toward her. But Adrianna wouldn't come forth with whatever it was that bugged her about Justine. So Justine felt as though her hands were tied.

Because Justine felt less and less in control over the situation, after a few months she became less and less responsible at work. She began arriving late and leaving early. Although she was generally an honest and trustworthy person, she even resorted to asking her coworkers to clock her in and out so she could avoid getting docked any pay. She also started having a bad attitude with the customers.

When Justine came to my office, she was a wreck. She had been losing sleep and feeling anxious all the time because of her work situation. She hated going to work every day, and despite having had a pretty positive self-image, she was starting to doubt her self-worth. Though I never met Adrianna and heard her personal story, it seemed pretty clear to me that Adrianna was most likely caught in a transference trap with Justine. And Justine's increasing irresponsibility suggested a countertransference trap in action.

Through exploration of Justine's family background, we came to understand a similarity between Adrianna's behavior and that of Joe, her older brother. Joe had one of those charming personalities that brought him a lot of popularity with the parents and his peers. However, behind the scenes, he treated Justine disrespectfully and sometimes even abusively. He would call her "pig face" and tell her she was fat. The minute anyone else would show up, he'd put a big smile on his face and hug Justine to demonstrate his "genuine" love for her. You got it—he was Mister Two-Face in action.

Unbeknownst to Justine, the dynamic she faced at work—of her boss behaving kindly toward everyone but her—pressed on this deep emotional bruise that originated out of her relationship with her brother. But once she discovered the countertransference in play, Justine was able to return to work without acting irresponsibly. However, given that Adrianna's behavior continued to be irrational, Justine eventually made the decision to look for another job.

If you're anything like me, you're probably wondering what was going on with Adrianna that made her behave this way toward

Justine. I wish I could tell you, but neither Justine nor I were ever privy to Adrianna's history and whatever bruises she endured. The good news, though, is that we don't have to know where someone else's transference originates in order to get a handle on our own reactions to it.

Identifying countertransference helps make us more capable of staying on top of our choices, especially at work. Clearly, it can't erase the transference that originates with someone else, but it gives us more choices in terms of how we elect to respond to it. Sometimes other people's behavior toward us will be unbearable, regardless of whether we've fully recovered from our own bruises. But often, once we've eliminated our countertransference reaction, the transference has much less power.

## Not All Reactions Are Created Equal

It's important to understand that not all of the reactions we have to others are transference, nor are all responses to transference considered to be countertransference. Sometimes we have emotional responses and behaviors that are completely appropriate to an interaction. Basically, countertransference and transference reactions include at least one of the following five conditions:

1. They're not conscious.
2. They stem from childhood experiences.
3. They're the product of involuntary reactions, rather than deliberate choices.
4. They're bigger or more intense than are appropriate to the situation.
5. They cause a regression from adultlike behavior (i.e., responsible, deliberate, and professional) to more child-like behavior (i.e., reactive, impulsive, self-centered, whiny, helpless).

After a few months of counseling, Tori had learned how to manage her transference and countertransference reactions pretty well.

Though she had a pretty full suitcase from childhood, once she recognized that many of her reactions stemmed from old bruises, she was able to find ways to calm herself down when her buttons got pushed and then deal with the feelings more appropriately later on. In doing so, she kept her professionalism intact. Just by becoming more conscious of these old feelings, and how they got triggered, she became much more in charge of her own behavior.

Please note that this doesn't mean we won't still behave the same way once we understand our transference and countertransference. For instance, Jackie's boss, Rebecca, treated Jackie like dirt and put her down constantly. Jackie couldn't stand Rebecca, and all of Jackie's coworkers felt sorry for her. Clearly, Rebecca was having some kind of transference toward Jackie. Most likely Rebecca felt threatened by Jackie; maybe she even feared that Jackie might one day get her job.

Rebecca's behavior resembled that of a former best friend that Jackie had during elementary school. Jackie and this girl, Cindy, had a falling out in fifth grade, when Cindy had accused Jackie of gossiping about her to another one of their friends. Cindy refused to listen to Jackie's side of the story, and basically she shunned Jackie throughout junior high—at times really being cruel to Jackie.

Jackie had learned during junior high that the best way to deal with Cindy was to ignore her comments and provocative gestures. She learned to develop a very thick skin around her.

Once in the workplace and encountering Rebecca, Jackie applied similar techniques to handle this relationship. At first, her behavior stemmed from fear, but as she came to work through this old bruise incurred in the fifth grade, she came to conclude that ignoring Rebecca was still the preferred style. In fact, she tried asserting herself, and this seemed to only make matters worse. Since she really enjoyed her job, she made peace with the fact that while she had no power over Rebecca's behavior, she could still *choose* to not let it affect her. In this situation, it worked best for her to maintain her thick skin and find ways to manipulate the situation to her advantage. She no longer operated out of countertransference— because she was conscious and aware of her options.

► *Transference Hunt Exercise*

Since you never know when you might trip into another transference trap, it's always useful to have a systematic method for getting untangled.

But before you plunge into the following exercise, make sure that you have ample time to participate with no distractions. If this isn't the best time, then you'll be better off coming back to this later rather than attempting to rush through it now. Plus, remember that learning is a *process*. This is not something you just do once and then forget about. Don't expect to accomplish this particular exercise all in one sitting.

At first, you may have to apply these steps after the workday is long over, or on weekends when you're not right in the throes of whatever is getting you all fired up. With some practice, and the greater awareness that will come with it, you'll be able to identify and eliminate any transference before it causes you too much distress or leads you to misbehave. Eventually, you will be able to cut transference off at the pass before it has any power at all. So get ready—you're going on a transference hunt.

**Step One:** Create some distance between yourself and your transference. Remember that transference reactions stem from your old stuff. So, even if you're currently in a toxic situation, you'll have a hard time handling it effectively if transference has been activated. Thus, take a step back from the emotional intensity you're feeling. I recommend that you picture yourself as a journalist reporting on a very important story. This will help you develop a more objective take on what's happening.

**Step Two:** Make a list of the people in your workplace with whom you think you have ever had transference or countertransference reactions, either positive or negative—though for the time being, I'd recommend you spend more of your energy on that which has caused negative reactions. Remember, anyone in the workplace can trigger transference, including your boss (if you have one), co-workers, clients, or staff. They may be older or younger, of the same or opposite gender. For each person on the list, write out a description of what feelings or behaviors get triggered in you and some examples of how this has shown up.

**Step Three:** Make a list of all the important people who had an influence on your emotional development in your childhood. Consider all prospects, including, but not limited to, immediate family members (parents, stepparents, siblings), other relatives (grandparents, uncles, aunts, cousins), teachers, mentors, babysitters, friends, and peers. You might even add the general category of society, including things like the media and prevailing cultural norms, to the list.

If you endured some sort of isolated trauma, like a single-incident assault, make sure to include anybody whose involvement left a mark on your memory. For instance, Eleanor, a twentysomething dental assistant, had endured the horrific experience of rape at age seventeen. Though she never saw the rapist again following the assault, his image was indelibly imprinted in her mind. Because of transference, she later realized, she sometimes reacted with fear to the dentist whom she worked for, because his voice quality resembled that of her assailant. Clearly, her attacker was present for only a fraction of time relative to many other people in her life, yet because of the trauma he caused, he turned out to have a terrible impact in terms of how she had to cope with transference. Similarly, for people who've been molested by someone outside the immediate family—even if this just happened one time—whatever is left unhealed can become the basis for transference.

**Step Four:** Next to each person's name you've identified in Step Three, describe which of your old bruises you associate with that person. Try to be as specific as possible. Think of things like needs that weren't met, expectations that were disappointed, and poor connections because of differences in personality dynamics.

As you work on this step, keep in mind that a wound is a wound is a wound. As you've already learned, in order to finally get past your old stuff, you can't get caught up in rationalizing other people's behavior that hurt you, even if it was unintentional. Plus, the goal is neither to assign blame to others nor to yourself. Rather, it's about letting people be accountable for their share of the responsibility. You need only to be accountable for your actions in adulthood—no more, no less.

I've found that the best way to facilitate this process is to distinguish what is truly our own responsibility from things that were influenced by someone else. And in childhood, most if not all of our actions are influenced by others. Why? Because as children, our ability to make our own choices—about whom we spend time with, what we do, and how we behave—is very limited. Thus, it's very important to let go of any responsibility you're holding onto for things that happened to you, or feelings you experienced, that ultimately belonged with someone else. You need to throw in the trash whatever stuff you're carrying that was dumped on you by someone else. Fortunately, you don't even need to call the garbage collector. Once it's out of you, it will disintegrate!

**Step Five:** Now, revisit your list of people in your workplace. Using your cast of characters from your past, try to identify which people from your workplace remind you of which people from your emotional history.

You can have more than one association per person on the list, with multiple combinations. For instance, your boss might triggers transference traps involving old bruises stemming from both your mom and your dad. Your coworker might unconsciously remind you of both a teacher and a sibling or other family member. Or a client triggers old stuff you associate with a babysitter and a cousin, and even a little bit of mom. The possibilities are far too numerous to mention, so be creative in your thinking and know that anything is possible.

**Step Six:** It's time to let go of the past and cut the cord once and for all. But to do so you must make a commitment to live in the present and vow to take care of yourself. By virtue of making this vow, you significantly reduce the possibility of other people having the power to push your buttons. This sends a signal to the world that you like and value yourself. You're also posting a sign (metaphorically, that is) that there's a certain boundary that no one has permission to cross. (I can't tell you exactly how this mechanism works, but over the past twenty years, for me at least, it's never failed.)

For the next several months, keep a journal handy wherever you go. Each time you recognize something creeping up that has roots in your past, write it down. Later in the day or evening, when you have some downtime, revisit the journal and review what you've written. Say aloud the following: "I understand that this past experience has lingered on because I've not yet let it go. But from today forward I promise to recognize that this is old stuff, and I have the power to make my experience more positive in the present." By making this statement, you are putting into action the concept of embracing choice and responsibility. This may seem like a tedious process. But isn't it more tedious to be burdened by the weight of a ball and chain? So please, put in the time and energy required to realize this new empowerment over your own life. It will be well worth it in the end.

The key to your success is to be willing to do whatever it takes to let go of old stuff. If that means you need professional counseling, then okay, that's what you need to get. Or if it means that you need to read much more about subjects like learning self-love and healing old bruises, then go for it. Basically, if you want to do what it takes to stop contributing to drama in your workplace, you have to be proactive. Thus, you need to do whatever it takes to make this step happen. And I assure you that you'll be very happy with the results.

You must *own* the fact that you're not a victim of your life—you're the master of it. As an adult—like every other adult—you have choices that you didn't have as a child. You have the power to assert these choices. From this standpoint, you are only a victim if you have no, and I mean NO, choices—that is, when someone or some circumstance has truly stripped you of all your power, and you are helpless. Otherwise—even if you think all of your options stink—if you have any power to choose, then you're not a victim. Staying stuck in your childhood keeps you a victim. So please, make the choice—*choose* to thrive instead.

# Seven

STEP FOUR—

# How to Separate Your Old Stuff from the Truly Intolerable

As you probably already know, it's always much easier to blame other people for our distress than to look at our own selves under a microscope. But I hope you're coming to recognize that, in the end, you'll reap much greater benefit from your efforts to improve your situation if you keep the primary focus on *yourself*—i.e., on understanding the roots of your own feelings and behavior, and claiming your power to make changes when your choices aren't working. Nevertheless, because it can be so difficult to stay attentive solely to the hard work of confronting your own challenges and issues, I want to propose a quick exercise to help you to get more immediate results.

Let's start off with an imagery exercise. For the next five minutes, close your eyes and take several long, deep breaths. As you inhale, imagine taking in positive energy. Visualize yourself as someone who is successful and happy in the workplace. As you exhale, imagine that you are letting go of all your old stuff. You might picture yourself tossing it out into a big garbage can. If you don't like that image, pick another one. Meanwhile, as you're dumping, say to yourself, "I don't need to hold onto things that no longer exist." Or if it suits your personality better, you could say something more like, "Bye-bye crap, hello good times!" The specific words you use don't matter so much as long as they reflect genuine appreciation for your efforts, a welcoming in of nurturing energy, and a letting go of the negative.

Most importantly, relax and enjoy the moment. Whenever you find yourself getting stressed out about work, take a few minutes and practice this exercise. Over time, this tool of self-care should become more like an automatic reflex. When you're ready, move on to the next section of this book, where we'll address how to distinguish between problems at work created by your old stuff cooking up trouble, and problems created by other people behaving in ways that are truly intolerable.

## Identifying "Out-of-Bounds" Behaviors

Though I most definitely stand behind my view that being responsible for yourself is the key to happiness and success, I also wholeheartedly understand that certain people behave in ways that can push almost anyone's buttons. Sometimes, even after sorting out transference and countertransference, you'll still find someone else's behavior to be truly unbearable. And, quite frankly, so too would most other people, regardless of their individual histories. So, I'm now inviting you to examine, *briefly*, the behavior of others and to evaluate its appropriateness in the workplace. Of course, all the while, I still encourage you to pay attention to your own participation in any given interaction.

Below is a list of what I call "out-of-bounds" behaviors. To be considered out of bounds, these behaviors must meet two criteria: 1) they would be toxic and inappropriate in any workplace environment, and 2) most people would agree that they're toxic. While this is still a very subjective definition, I think it will give you a workable framework from which to determine whether the problems you're encountering in your workplace are the product of your old stuff or largely the result of someone else's behavior.

Naturally, some people will always be able to rationalize or justify the merits of these behaviors. Thus, you can't judge for certain whether something is inappropriate or not based on just a few other opinions. That's why it's important that the behavior be considered inappropriate by many. And even if these behaviors stem from transference or countertransference, they don't belong in the office. So if you're thinking that a behavior is truly intolerable, run the description by some of your most honest friends or loved ones, and see what they think.

Remember, while the focus in this chapter is on other people's behavior, don't be surprised if you recognize yourself in any of these descriptions. After all, none of us is perfect. All of us are subject to misbehaving now and again, even to the point of being out of bounds. Try to acknowledge what you discover, take responsibility for it, and then make a concerted effort to modify your behavior. As you've learned, with awareness and commitment you become more empowered to choose different behaviors.

### The Verbal Abuser

Some people act like loose cannons regardless of the circumstances. Whether provoked or not, they verbally attack anyone in their path. Verbal abuse shows no favoritism to status within a workplace environment. You might encounter such behavior from the boss, a coworker, a client, or even a subordinate. However, most often you'll find that a verbal abuser will show more restraint when it comes to the boss, for obvious reasons.

Full-fledged verbal abusers show no mercy. Their behavior cannot be explained away by an occasional bad mood, PMS, or migraine headache. The behavior is pervasive, frequent, intentional, and consistently toxic.

Verbal assault may come in the form of name-calling: "You're such an idiot." Or, "You lazy-ass, who hired you for this job?"

Or, the abuser may hurl insults: "My grandmother could finish that project in her sleep faster than you can even on ten cups of coffee." Or, "You're never going to amount to anything in this company."

The assault may be covert but equally stinging. For instance, Hilary worked side by side with Summer, who constantly criticized her every effort. Summer would say things like, "Hey Hilary, I hope you don't have anywhere to go tonight, because at the pace you work, you'll be here until next Friday." In fact, Hilary wasn't a slow worker at all—Summer just said these things to put her down and make her feel bad about herself.

Verbally abusive individuals tend to disregard the rights and feelings of others, and they tend to feel entitled to say whatever they want without consequences. Verbal abusers often use others as receptacles into which they dump their own frustrations. Often, abusive people also treat themselves with the same disregard. Whenever they make a mistake or fail to meet a personal standard, they badger themselves just as cruelly. But don't let this sway you into making excuses for the abuser's behavior. Committing the same crime toward oneself doesn't make it okay to do to others. After all, we've all been taught that two wrongs don't make a right!

Alison's boss, Mark, constantly barked at his staff. Whether he was in a good or bad mood, whether he had eaten breakfast or not, or whether he'd just completed a project on time or was consumed with fear that he would miss an approaching deadline—none of these things seemed to matter. No one could detect any rhyme or reason to his foul moods. He ranted and raved on a daily basis.

At first, Alison took his behavior personally. She believed that it was her inadequate performance that made her deserving of Mark's attacks. She would go home each night and cry on her husband's shoulder, feeling like a failure. Not surprisingly, Mark's style elicited transference in Alison, since her mom was similarly volatile. But this wasn't the whole story. Though the *intensity* of Alison's reaction to Mark could be pegged on transference, that didn't change the fact that Mark's behavior was obnoxious. Thus, regardless of Alison's past, which skewed her perception at times, her boss's behavior was truly out of bounds. He was the jerk. She wasn't in any way a failure.

Even the most emotionally healthy people in Alison's office were affected by Mark's behavior. While some were able to brush him off more easily, referring to him as "the ass" and laughing off his abuse, many others were thrown off balance. In fact, Mark's staff had the highest turnover rate within the company, and he produced the lowest office morale. You'd think he would have been fired, but hey—wouldn't you know it?—he was the company owner's cousin.

Though verbal abusers may try to convince you that they're entitled to behave the way they do, their behavior is unacceptable and shouldn't be tolerated. No one deserves to be badgered, bullied, or belittled. You could actually *choose* to stay in a workplace environment with a verbal abuser, provided you can maintain your emotional balance without being rocked or swayed by the insults. But if the abuser's negative energy seeps in even a tiny bit and gets the best of you, you must eject the bad feelings that seep in, if the job seems worth it. Or you could make the decision to leave that job. As long as you're in charge of your decisions and don't feel controlled by the abuser, you can basically ignore the abuse.

By the way, if you work with someone who fits this description, you have other choices besides confronting the abuser or quitting your job. Remember, the key to creating healthy relationships involves simply being aware of what's really going on and making *choices* about how to behave.

Consider the dynamic between Dana and Trudy. Trudy, Dana's coworker, felt threatened by Dana's success. No matter how nice Dana would be toward her, Trudy insulted Dana at every opportunity. Sometimes she would be downright mean. She'd say "You really know how to suck up to the boss to get ahead, don't you?" Or, she'd be more subtly demeaning by saying, "I guess we all can't be so lucky to be blessed with a silver spoon." Mind you, Dana was an exceptionally hard-working and ethical gal. She would never even consider resorting to any tactics to get ahead other than hard work. Trudy, however, couldn't accept that Dana was legitimately making her mark at the company. Because of envy, Trudy went out of her way to put Dana down.

Initially, Dana felt she had no options other than wringing Trudy's neck or quitting her job. But while Dana had a hard time deciding how to proceed, she could handle Trudy's insults after she learned more about how her own buttons were being pushed, and how to prevent them from getting pushed in the first place. She discovered that by strengthening her self-confidence and building better emotional boundaries, she could mostly ignore Trudy and just go about her work, not taking personally any of Trudy's comments.

Of course, you have to be careful in determining whether someone you work with is a true verbal abuser. It's possible that if you are sensitive to being judged or are easily shamed, you may have a hard time taking legitimate suggestions and feedback. You might be prone to perceiving any type of evaluation as harsh criticism, insults, or attacks. Yes, you got it—you might be stuck in a transference trap.

Rebecca grew up in a family where everyone had to fend for themselves. There were six kids, all between one to three years apart in age. Her mom and dad both worked outside the home, and there wasn't a whole lot of time for one-on-one attention. Rebecca, the third from the eldest, felt as though she never fit in. In fact, she spent much of her childhood fantasizing about her "biological parents." No, she wasn't adopted; she just believed she must have been, since she seemed to have nothing in common with her parents or siblings.

Being a more sensitive type who'd felt like an outsider in her own family, Rebecca entered the workforce unconsciously looking for a replacement dad or mom. She hoped she would be seen as a star, for once in her life, and never disappoint anyone again. Of course, these feelings weren't realistic, but they guided her behavior nonetheless.

After college, Rebecca got a job in an accounting firm, where she worked on the books for some pretty prestigious clients. On a few occasions, Rebecca made some big mistakes that were quite costly. Her boss, Carter, was understandably upset. He pointed out that Rebecca had made some grave errors that couldn't happen again should she wish to keep her job. Rebecca wasn't able to handle this criticism. She believed that Carter was treating her unfairly. It wasn't until she was able to get a grip on her emotional bruises from childhood that she was able to see just how unreasonable it was to categorize her boss as mean. Carter had every right to expect precise accounting work from her, and he had every right to express his concern when her work fell short. It wasn't his job to fix the holes in Rebecca's self-esteem.

The moral of this story is, if you believe you work with a verbal abuser, first make sure you've attended to all your transference and that you're not overreacting to legitimate feedback. Then, once you've determined it's not you, take action toward doing what's best for you.

## The Yeller

People who need to raise their voice in order to make their point tend to lose their listeners fairly quickly, even if they're not saying anything particularly hostile or angry. This behavior keeps people at a distance and sometimes can be abusive. I'm not talking about someone whose voice goes up a notch or two in emphasis. I am talking about the type of screamer who everybody in the building can hear even with the doors closed.

Yellers lack impulse control when it comes to their sense of frustration. Many learned in their own childhoods that yelling was the only way to be heard or to get attention. Naturally they keep this survival mechanism up in the workplace, but not without serious consequences. They might be saying something quite appropriate, but the message gets lost because of the too-loud delivery.

To determine whether a yeller you work with is truly intolerable requires close examination of your own history. The trick here is to distinguish what's simply an animated tone from what's outright yelling. Many people with loud voices can be misperceived as threatening, especially when they're angry, since we often associate loudness with the onset of an attack—even a physical attack. But just because someone is loud doesn't mean they are intolerable, nor does it mean that they need to be feared. However, if someone uses the volume of his or her voice to bully or intimidate others, then this should be considered intolerable behavior.

If you've endured any kind of abuse in your history, you might be prone to perceiving a raised tone of voice as louder and more threatening than it actually is. Conversely, with the same history, you might have become desensitized to noticing when someone else's volume is over the top. In the former situation, you might be likely to feel threatened even when there is no sign of actually danger. And in the latter, you might be so immune to the loudness that you fail to notice even when danger might be present. You would be prone to denying the toxicity of the yelling, though your body would continue to be disturbed.

Melanie's older brother had commanded all the family's attention through his temper tantrums. The louder he became, the more he got his way. Later on, when Melanie got a job at a home electronics store, she encountered a coworker similar to her brother. But Melanie had become so used to this negative energy that she didn't even think to identify it as a possible cause of all these other symptoms she was having: trouble sleeping, anxiety, and jitteriness. She also gained weight from constantly grazing on cookies and candy in an effort to numb out from the stress she experienced on the job.

Melanie had no idea that these reactions had anything to do with the similarity between her coworker's tantrums and those of her brother's. She thought she had grown immune to being affected by such behavior. However, she eventually learned that even though she tried to ignore the impact the yelling had on her, it affected her nonetheless. Once she made the connection, she talked to her boss about her coworker's behavior. Unfortunately, Melanie's boss failed to take any action, and Melanie opted to find another job.

## The Backstabber

I think we've all met one or two of these types, even though they can be quite hard to spot at first. Actually, backstabbers often appear wrapped in very nice packages. They approach you with smiley faces and offerings of help. Sometimes they might seem really generous by doing unasked-for favors to make your life on the job easier. But beware! Backstabbers are vicious and highly manipulative. They don't have your best interest at heart. Back-stabbers watch to see where your vulnerabilities are so they can get you when you're weak. They want you to fail, and they may go to any length to sabotage your work or steal your job. They will lie, cheat, or steal if it gives them a better chance to get ahead.

One cannot have a positive relationship with a backstabber. It's simply not possible. They're not trustworthy. Whereas with the verbal abuser or the yeller, you may be able to preserve some civility when they're not behaving irrationally, with the backstabber, there's no chance.

Backstabbers can be so difficult to spot because they do their dirty work behind the scenes, so you often don't know you're being victimized. A backstabber may repeatedly "forget" to convey important information to you to enable you to do your job. Or she may fail to inform you of a crucial company meeting, or even take credit for your work. Mind you, I certainly don't want to promote unfounded paranoia, nor do I mean to suggest that you distrust everyone in your workplace. But it's good to know that these people exist so that you're not completely taken aback if you discover that you've got one of these outside your office door.

So how do you defend yourself from someone whose out-of-bounds behavior is grounded in outright deception? Generally speaking, the more confident you grow in trusting your gut, the better you'll become at spotting backstabbers and their methods of subterfuge. And the better you are at maintaining solid, healthy boundaries with your coworkers, the less likely you'll be to get nailed by a backstabber in the first place.

Jimmy earned his living as a graphic artist, and quite a well-respected one at that. A few years ago, he found a new job where he was hired to supervise a whole division. Jimmy was certainly capable of handling the responsibility, though it quickly became evident that one of his team members, Haley, felt cheated that she hadn't gotten the position instead. To make matters worse, the president of the company had assigned Haley to show Jimmy the ropes during the first few months of his employment. Well, she sure did. She showed him the rope to hang himself with.

Haley, of course, didn't reveal her true colors right off the bat. Instead, she started by charming Jimmy. She acted as if she were delighted by his arrival and had him believing that he was a welcome addition to the team. But before long, Jimmy began to notice that he wasn't being given important information, the lack of which almost cost him his job. And all fingers pointed toward Haley as the culprit.

After a couple of *years* spent trying to work around Haley's attempts to destroy his success, Jimmy recognized that he didn't have the power he needed to make his situation better at his workplace. He wasn't getting the support he required from those in higher positions. He accepted that if anything were to improve it would be from him finding another job. Once he was out of that crazy situation for a little while, he could more easily spot many other signs of dysfunction throughout the whole company. No wonder Haley had gotten away with her bad behavior for so long. Fortunately, Jimmy learned how to take better care of himself, and he eventually found a job within a much healthier organization.

If you believe you've been targeted by a backstabber, do what you can to eliminate any power she has over you by taking assertive action on your own behalf. For instance, appropriately inform your boss of the situation, or go through human resources. Don't rely on the backstabber to be a conduit for any important information. And always check the information the backstabber gives you against information from others in the company. If you don't get the support you need from those higher up in order to deal with the backstabber, you have to make a decision as to whether you'd be better off somewhere else.

Whatever you do, don't waste your energy on revenge or countersubterfuge. Backstabbers rarely ever come clean and take responsibility for their behavior. You'll be fighting a losing battle if you attempt to make them understand or feel sorry for what they've done to you. After all, if they were empathetic, compassionate people, they wouldn't be backstabbers. The more you focus on their behavior, the more they tend to feel entitled to their manipulations. They may even try to convince you that you're victimizing them. You're better off working around them or getting out.

## The Discriminator

Discrimination, whether based on age, gender, race, religious affiliation, or other criteria, is not only unprofessional—it's illegal. While most everyone holds a prejudice or two in their minds, we need to work hard to understand where our biases come from and refrain from allowing these pre-judgments to rule our behavior. No matter how much we may fear difference in someone else, or be threatened by it, we should never let these fears lead us to mistreat others. Anyone who acts out their prejudices by treating people unfairly should not be tolerated.

If you come across a discriminator, don't have high hopes that this person will ever become enlightened. Rather, figure out how you can either take action to stop the discrimination or remove yourself from the situation.

## The Rule-Breaker

There's always someone in every group, it seems, who thinks the rules don't apply to her. I don't mean someone who occasionally shows up late or calls in sick when she's really off playing hooky at the beach. I mean the type who constantly marches to the beat of her own drum. This is particularly upsetting if this rule-breaker is the boss and she asserts a double standard—i.e., she expects everyone else to follow the rules while she's breaking them all.

Rule-breakers often expect others to do more than their fair share—and to make matters worse, the extra that's done goes unnoticed. They may even go so far as to violate state or federal employment laws—not allowing you to take a lunch break, requiring that you work overtime without compensation, or docking you earned vacation time because you didn't get an assignment in on time.

Rule-breakers can become quite indignant if they're busted,

blaming others for why they do what they do, or even acting ignorant about the actual letter of the law. Rule-breakers often have no remorse and don't have any true awareness of how important it is to set and maintain effective rules in the workplace. They will often rely on emotional blackmail to get others to protect them from being outed.

If you work for or with a rule-breaker, before you decide whether her behavior is truly intolerable, ask yourself the following questions:

- "Does this person's behavior affect how well I can do my job?"
- "Am I also being forced to break the rules?"
- "Does the type of rule-breaking involved violate my code of morals and ethics?"

If you're able to answer "no" to all three questions, then you might be able to tolerate a rule-breaker as long as you maintain good protective boundaries and watch your back. But be careful about working for any company that condones rule-breaking. You most likely won't be treated very fairly—nor will you necessarily be admired for abiding by the codes. In fact, you might be viewed as uptight or a Goody Two-shoes. It's always best to find work in an environment that supports your own value system. Otherwise, you'll end up in a chronic state of stress, which we all know isn't good for our mind, body, or soul.

## The Physical Assaulter

Any aggressive act or any threat of bodily harm constitutes intolerable behavior. No one should ever have to fear intentional physical injury in the workplace.

If you have ever been met with violence in the workplace, you know how scary it can be. In the moment, you must do whatever it takes to remove yourself from physical danger as quickly as possible, and then take action to ensure you're never in that position again. All companies should have a zero-tolerance policy against acts or threats of violence.

Sometimes people forgive acts of violence that don't actually culminate in direct physical contact with another person. For instance, some people demonstrate aggression by slamming doors, beating their fists on a table, or throwing inanimate objects. But even these expressions of aggression can intimidate others, and they have no place in the office. Obviously, we must all allow for variation in how we express frustration and anger. But we also need to be able to respect how our behavior affects others. It's one thing to close the door to your office and scream into a pillow if your boss tells you that you won't be receiving a bonus you've been anticipating; it's a whole other story if you start throwing dishes around in the company kitchen after hearing this disappointing news.

Kirsten's boss was a fist-slammer. Whenever he was disappointed or frustrated, he would puff up like bear on steroids and start pounding on whatever surface was nearby. He didn't have to say a word to let people know when he was angry. In fact, it was clear to most people in the office that he was a ticking time bomb. Though he never actually violated anyone physically, the emotional terror he caused was sufficient to warrant disciplinary intervention. Kirsten eventually went to the president of the company and voiced a complaint. Fortunately for Kirsten, her boss was ultimately terminated.

While some people might have greater tolerance for this kind of behavior, it shouldn't be condoned. If you're in a workplace environment where this behavior is ignored or forgiven, I highly recommend that you seek employment elsewhere. As I've already noted, our bodies become very stressed in this type of emotional climate; why would you want to subject yourself to such discomfort when you don't have to?

## The Sexual Assaulter

I will go into more detail concerning sexual harassment in Chapter Ten. But for now, it's important for you to understand that this is one of the most intolerable behaviors in the workplace. Sexual assault comes in many forms, including inappropriate remarks or advances, sexual blackmail (which can include promising someone extra favors if they put out sexually), groping, swats on the butt, and other unwanted personal touching. However, although all sexual behavior should be off limits in the workplace, it's good to keep in mind that all sexual behavior doesn't constitute sexual harassment.

Sometimes we inadvertently or even consciously invite sexual behavior from our coworkers. Because this is a very sensitive topic, you need to examine your situation very carefully if you're feeling violated in this way. Ultimately, we all need to be very thoughtful about the messages we send out to our coworkers. While I am in no way blaming the victim, it has been my experience that in certain situations, inappropriate sexual advances might never have been made if someone had been more aware of how her old stuff was affecting her workplace behavior. Let me explain through an example.

Sophia had been molested as a child. As is common among young girls who have been molested, Sophia became sexually promiscuous in her teens and twenties. As she developed more self-respect and went through a process of uncovering and healing the wounds that resulted from her experiences, she became more and more aware of the messages she was sending out into the world. She began noticing that her body language, style of dress, and general demeanor of low self-esteem were actually signaling that she was receptive to unwanted advances. That's not to say that anyone had any right to cross Sophia's boundaries, but she became acutely aware that she definitely had a role in the energy she was sending out.

With her new awareness, Sophia began to dress more conservatively (although still quite stylishly) and developed more of a "don't-mess-with-me" attitude, while continuing to maintain her pleasant and kind demeanor. Rather than getting unwanted sexual attention, she soon found herself being treated with much greater respect.

There's a fine line between being a victim of sexual attention and unwittingly inviting it. I think it's very important to define that line as clearly and precisely as possible. If you have been subjected to unwanted sexual advances, take a really close look at the unconscious messages you give off. If something happens to us once as an isolated experience, it's quite likely that it's a fluke. But if you start noticing a pattern, there's a good chance that you can do something to prevent more of these situations from developing.

### ▸ *Out of Bounds Exercise*

So what's on your list of truly intolerable, boundary-busting behaviors? Try to identify the ways in which you yourself have behaved outside of the bounds. Next, examine how others may have crossed these lines. Go through all the significant players in your workplace, and think about their behavior. If you notice that you have a coworker or boss who behaves in these inappropriate ways, try to assess whether you think there are creative ways that you might be able to deal more effectively with the situation. If you think it's hopeless, start thinking about a plan to leave.

Again, I want to emphasize that there is rarely a right or wrong answer when it comes to addressing any given situation. There are simply too many variables in play. What's most important is that you stay conscious and thoughtful, always attentive to taking responsibility where it's really yours and letting go of the rest. This is your life, and only you can decide what you can live with or not.

If you determine that it would be better to move on, do so with integrity. Regardless of whether someone else acts out of bounds, unless you're in a life-or-death situation, you almost always have the option to behave sensibly. I recommend you always assert this option if you can.

## Guidelines for Addressing Out-of-Bounds Behavior

- First and foremost, always try to follow company protocol. Every employer should provide a handbook that includes a description of how to proceed if you feel as though workplace rules or regulations have been violated. Clearly, if you work for a very small firm or in an independent setting, this may not be so formalized. However, even in a business arrangement where it's just you and a boss, there should be some understanding of your rights as an employee, even if it's only communicated verbally. You can always contact the state or U.S. Department of Labor with any additional questions.

- It's usually best to go the route of highest civility first, unless you have clear-cut evidence that the perpetrator won't respond in a rational way. Save "fighting fire with fire" for the most extreme cases when you have no other options.
- If you go through all the appropriate channels—and you're certain you've distinguished your old stuff from truly intolerable behavior—you can always proceed with legal intervention, or you can opt to find another job. Or both.
- If you decide it's best to leave, empower yourself by understanding that *you* are making the choice to better your situation in the long run, even if it might make your life a bit harder in the present.
- Above all, honor your decision to make your life better!

Your emotional well-being needs to be a priority. If you determine that your situation is truly unbearable, make it a priority to do whatever it takes to move on as quickly as possible. Of course, you need to plan any move you make in a sound and rational fashion. It's probably not wise to bail out on your job, unless something truly awful happens, until you have a solid plan in place for finding new employment. Time and time again, though, I've seen people terrified of leaving a situation only to discover that once they actually take the plunge, they've opened the door to many more new and exciting opportunities. Sometimes we get comfortable with what's familiar to us, no matter how awful, and we fear making changes. However, if we stay stuck in this mentality, we stunt our growth. So think hard, do a proper cost-benefit analysis, and be sure to factor in your emotional sanity in making your decision to stay or go.

This is all very difficult stuff to sort out. But three cheers for you! You've made it over yet another hurdle. And because of your dedication, you have even better tools for how to approach the trials and tribulations that we all encounter in the workplace.

▸ *Progress Exercise*

Please pause to acknowledge your progress. Take a moment to appreciate whatever steps you've taken thus far to improve your life. Affirm that you are making strides toward your goals. C'mon, don't hold back. Let out your sense of pride and appreciation. After all, how often do we get to shine the light on our own positive behavior? So do it when you can. You should applaud yourself for your commitment and dedication to self-discovery. Don't just accept my praise. Congratulate yourself. It's very important to recognize our own gains and progress.

Please don't brush this suggestion off. Scrutinizing our own behavior can be enormously taxing. We all need ongoing positive reinforcement to provide the fuel needed to energize our momentum. So keep up that good self-care by actively acknowledging your willingness to be challenged and to keep plunging forward.

▶ *Eight*

STEP FIVE—
# Transcend Power Struggles

In this chapter, we're going to tackle power struggles. Even if you determine that your present workplace is so screwed up you have to find another job, you can still benefit from learning how to transcend power struggles. After all, *no* workplace is perfect. Power struggles will be inevitable wherever you go until you get a handle on dealing with them.

Doing so requires you to learn how to maintain the utmost professionalism in any workplace environment. (Don't worry, this doesn't mean you also have to be completely serious—the workplace can and should also have time for fun!) So, whether you're soon moving on to a new position or company, have already started a new job, or have decided to stay where you are, you can begin applying many of these tools right away, and in doing so take steps to eliminate the drama in your workplace.

As you read on, however, keep in mind that old habits are hard to break. Hence, I encourage you to be patient. After all, getting involved in power struggles can be quite alluring. It's easy to get seduced into a conflict, even when you've become free of transference and countertransference. So if you find yourself still getting engaged by these kinds of conflicts, try to remember that you can always disengage the moment you recognize that you've stepped into a booby trap.

Also, I want to underline an important principle concerning the maintenance of sanity. Basically, no matter how hard you try, and how emotionally free of old stuff you become, you can only stay sane within an insane environment for so long. Craziness will eventually rule and get the best of anyone. Because of this basic principle, and the pervasive toxicity of workplaces dominated by out-of-bounds behavior, I caution you not to play "superhero." If you've determined that you are stuck in a situation that's truly intolerable, don't expect *any* of the tools outlined in this book to work all that well. These ideas can only be helpful in the short run, and they're only aimed at helping you improve yourself. In out-of-bounds situations, it's best to deal with things as rationally as possible until you're able to move on and find something better. Don't forget that once you assert your power to change your circumstances and remove yourself from a crazy situation, you can quickly regain your sanity.

Now let's move on to understanding power struggles, the parameters of our own power and control, the childhood stuff that predisposes us to get tangled in power struggles, and how to exercise as many options as possible within the bounds of our control.

## Power Struggles Defined

We often think of power struggles as what result when aggressive people fight for more control over something like territory or decision-making. And, yes this certainly describes a type of power struggle. However, just as with transference, power struggles come in all kinds of varieties and can occur among many different combinations of people, such as among coworkers, between coworkers and bosses, or between supervisors. They can happen among more than two people, and they can even occur solely within one's own mind, not even involving outside participants.

Though I can never say never concerning the usefulness of waging a power struggle, it's been my experience that such struggles can create needless drama and impede our success. Thus, regardless of how they get set in motion or who the combatants are, for the most part we don't need them. Hence, we should strive to eliminate them as best we can.

In order to help illustrate the power-struggle concept, I've provided these broad general descriptions of three basic types.

## Aggressor Meets Aggressor

In this scenario, we have two heavyweight prizefighters positioning themselves for a knockout. Even if there is a clear-cut winner, she will most likely be as bloody and worn down as her opponent by the time the bout is over. Unfortunately, the aftereffects of this kind of all-out workplace aggression often lead to the unemployment line.

People who engage in these kinds of take-no-prisoners battles tend to have domineering personalities, even when they're not actively engaged in a conflict. They also tend to be stubborn and self-righteous. Of course, these workplace aggressors aren't necessarily violent in physical terms. Nonetheless, the energy they give off can be very unpleasant and intimidating.

A more passive person may become this kind of an aggressor if she perceives that she's been backed into a corner with no way out. Under these conditions, even the gentle pussycat will lash out, clawing and biting, in a fight for survival.

Sybil and Jennifer constantly provoked one another. They competed for accolades from the same supervisor, and both felt threatened by the other's abilities. Sybil feared that Jennifer was after her job and vice versa. They each camouflaged their fear by trying to bully the other out of her point of view. Neither would ever budge from her position. Neither wanted to appear foolish for possibly being wrong, and neither ever wanted to appear vulnerable. As you might have guessed, these two were most likely ensnarled in a transference trap. And both were quite misguided as to what things were in their own control versus what weren't.

One day, their mutual aggression flared into physical violence when Sybil pushed Jennifer on the shoulder to get her out of her face. Not surprisingly, Jennifer pushed her right back. Fortunately a supervisor intervened before it got too ugly. But in the end, both put their jobs in jeopardy because they didn't know effective ways to deal with their stress. Needless to say, neither woman was going to get very far if they continued with this behavior.

## Avoider Meets Avoider

Another type of power struggle can happen with nonaggressive people. People who assert power through these means are sometimes known as *passive-aggressive*. Rather than directly voicing a particular stance or point of view, the passive-aggressive avoider only makes her feelings known covertly. She may do things like take a sick day when she's not even ill during a time when her team needs her most.

Anne and her boss, Carl, were stuck in this type of struggle. Carl would never come out and articulate his frustration with Anne's work when she failed to meet his expectations. He was too afraid of not being liked. Rather, he would assign tasks to other employees, even those who were less qualified. Anne would never be privy to the reasons why, but she would suspect that she had done something wrong in her boss's eyes. Anne was too intimidated to ask Carl directly about her performance. In an effort to get even, she would subtly make her boss's life more difficult by doing things like "accidentally" taking home files that he needed. To make matters worse, she would sulk and do even less-adequate work. From the outside looking in, Carl and Anne appeared like two children in a pouting war.

## Avoider Meets Aggressor

In these scenarios, one person uses passive means to advance her cause, while the other is more outwardly aggressive. In these cases, often the aggressor becomes even more visibly combative because she can't accept the limitations of her power. And the passive one retreats even more when she's around the aggressor because it's the only way she feels any sense of strength.

Christina tried to get the upper hand by directly attacking her coworker Jean. Christina would constantly order Jean around, even though she had no authority over her. Because Jean was so unassertive, she inadvertently became sucked into a power struggle. She would do things that ultimately sabotaged her own interests simply to keep Christina from getting her way. For instance, one day Christina criticized the way Jean was approaching a problem. To get even, Jean acted as if she were grateful to Christina for her input and said she would modify her approach; however, she actually turned in a flawed report instead, making herself look bad but also making Christina look bad, too. This further charged Christina's aggression, and she came down even harder on Jean.

Aggressive people tend to use bullying tactics in an effort to feel more in control. Avoiders, on the other hand, tend to use methods that may appear nonaggressive, but which can cause just as much damage. For instance, an avoider may forget to do an assignment, ultimately holding up the rest of the group, or she may withhold information that would allow other people to be more successful in their jobs. Usually the aggressor stays in the aggressive role, and the avoider maintains her avoidant position. But depending upon whose buttons get pushed, you might see a role reversal.

▸ *Struggle Style Exercise*

Now take a moment to assess whether you tend to get into power struggles, and, if so, with whom? Also, what's your dominant style—agressor or avoider? Make a list of your discoveries.

If you tend to be more of the aggressor, you need to work on toning it down and learning how to get your point across without trying to control others. If you tend to be more passive in your approach, you need to learn how to build your assertiveness skills. As you'll learn in the next section, a basic concept I've discussed throughout this book—how you need to recognize what kinds of things you have the power to control, and what kinds of things you can't—is also important when it comes to disengaging from power struggles.

## Understanding Your Power Parameters

By better understanding the parameters of your power, you'll learn how to set healthier boundaries with coworkers and bosses and how to transcend power struggles once and for all. You'll be better suited to make smart choices from among the options a given situation presents. If you don't understand your power parameters, you'll end up expending energy trying to fix the things you can't control and then not having enough left over to take care of your own responsibilities.

So, before we dive into my hands-on methods for how to transform power struggles, let's take a look at the parameters of power. First, you have to appreciate that the extent of your power, and the range of your choices, becomes either more or less limited depending on a) your goals, and b) what's happening around you.

Let me explain with an example. Let's say you discover that your boss repeatedly has unreasonable expectations of you. Well then, you certainly have the power to continue being reasonable while hoping for a different response from your boss. However, let's say your main, overarching professional goal is to keep yourself in a position where you're respected and treated fairly. In this case, given the inflexibility of your boss, it would not make sense for you to continue to waste energy trying to get your boss to see your point of view. Starting to see how this works? You still have power over your own choices, but because of your ultimate goal, your range of choices becomes more limited. Considering these conditions (specifically, this kind of boss), you would be better off getting out of your job unless you're willing to change that main goal. However, while the combination of your goal and your boss restricts your range of choices, you do still have some choices nonetheless. Remaining aware and attuned to all of your options keeps you from feeling like a victim.

Mind you, people who bring their old bruises into the workplace are often stuck in that victim/survivor mentality, believing that life happens to them rather than that they make their own lives happen. They are notorious for trying to control things that are totally out of their hands. Hence, they'll never be able to thrive. But not you! By recognizing and healing your old bruises, you're better able to recognize what you actually can control versus what's out of your hands. You will be more prepared to maintain smooth, peaceful, and mutually gratifying interactions with others, even when people all around you continue to be entwined in their own unhealthy patterns.

We are only *ever* in control of our own behavior, feelings, and thoughts. No matter how much we may wish to control other people's choices and reactions, we're out of luck. At best we might be able to create an illusion of being in control of others if they actually do what it is we want them to do. But, while we may have some influence on another person's behavior, ultimately each of us makes our own choices. Thus, the only thing we have real control over is ourselves.

Of course, another challenge is dealing with all of those *other* people who maintain a victim stance throughout their lives—those unfortunates who believe that their lives are solely the product of other people's choices for them. I certainly don't mean to sound unsympathetic to those who get wronged, mistreated, or violated. And certainly all of us, as children, had little or no control over the circumstances of our lives. (Of course, we have great power, influence, and most of all *responsibility* as parents, teachers, or care-givers of children and other true dependents who cannot care for themselves.) However, as adults, if we have embraced a pattern or mindset of being a victim, chances are that we are still respon-sible for any jeopardy that ensues, even though we perceive that it is others who are doing the harm. Basically, in adulthood, very rarely are we ever completely without any choices. Things happen to people—criminal acts, illnesses, acts of nature, freak occur-rences—but when it comes to our behavior, what we *do*, we must be accountable for our own choices.

Too often, people get caught up in trying to persuade or even coerce others to behave differently. Sometimes these methods work, especially if we've gone so far as to victimize someone so that they have no choice but to comply with our wishes. But these kinds of situations are at the very least dangerous, and at the worst outright criminal. In the workplace, our relationships with bosses, employees, and coworkers occur among independent, autonomous adults. Thus, we need to let others be responsible for their own choices and actions. And we need to stop spinning our wheels trying to get other people to change in an attempt to make ourselves feel better.

If you're trapped in this kind of negative spiral, it's time to nip it in the bud right now. Instead of reaching outward to feel in control, put your arms around yourself instead. In doing so, you're defining precisely the limits of your own power to change things. Believe me. I can't tell you how much of my own life I've wasted trying to get other people to see things my way. The last thing you need is to burden yourself with things you have no power to change.

As I've already noted, another part of understanding your power parameters is accepting your limitations. Sometimes our choices for our own selves become limited by the realities of the situation at hand. In other words, you might be taking the best possible care of yourself in a particular workplace relationship, yet because of how someone else is behaving, your choices become narrowed.

Arianna's partner on an important project, Shannon, failed to perform up to standards. In an ideal world, Shannon would have done equal work on their joint project, and she and Arianna would each have gotten their tasks done proficiently and efficiently. Or the boss would have seen the disparity in their efforts and taken action to remedy the imbalance. But neither was the case; in fact, no one intervened for over a year. Meanwhile, Shannon took really long lunch breaks, chatted with other coworkers constantly, and spent a lot of time surfing the internet rather than completing her share of the work.

At first, Arianna was infuriated. She was trying to earn a promotion and needed to produce excellent work. Arianna resented Shannon for not doing her fair share, but she was also well aware that the company frowned upon "tattletale-ing." Plus, the company had a reputation for finding ways to get rid of employees who complained too much. Arianna did everything she could to coax Shannon into pulling her weight, but to no avail. Arianna felt trapped.

What Arianna eventually discovered, however, was that she still had choices, even though none of her options looked very appealing at first. However, once she recognized that she didn't have the power to change Shannon's behavior, but that she did still have choices for how she could handle the situation, she felt more in control.

Arianna ultimately opted to do more than her fair share of the work, at least temporarily, because she really wanted to get the promotion for which she had been working so hard. She recognized that she could always quit if she wanted to, but that this would postpone her achieving her long-term goals. Thus, while Shannon's out-of-bounds behavior influenced the range of Arianna's choices, Arianna still had power over how to handle her part in the interaction.

## How Childhood Experiences Predispose Us to Power Struggles

It's impossible for me to delve too deeply here into the development of self-identity, as it would take several chapters (if not an entire book) to do justice to the topic. But it's certainly worth a few paragraphs to get a basic grasp on the role identity development plays in our workplace behavior.

You've probably heard the term "the terrible twos." Basically, this is the developmental process all children go through somewhere between the approximate ages of two through four, which is characterized by a constant verbalizing of the word "no." Essentially, this rebellion against authority helps a child develop her identity, establishing herself as a separate and unique being. There's nothing wrong with this. It's absolutely normal and a very healthy part of growing up.

Let's take a typical mother-toddler interaction. Mom asks her toddler to pick up a toy he just dropped. He looks Mom right in the eye with a big smile on his face and says "No!" She asks him again, and he says the same thing—only this time with even more animation while he giggles mischievously. He's not saying no to hurt his mom's feelings or necessarily to ruffle her feathers. Rather, he's relishing in his new discovery that his behavior produces consequences. This gives him a foundation for feeling secure and empowered. Of course, how he's handled in response to his rebelliousness will influence the course of his later self-development.

I think this phase got the rap of being "terrible" because it drives so many parents to the brink of wanting to trade in their kids for a well-trained dog. Not that they don't love their little naysayers, but a parent quickly becomes taxed by the constant challenges. In truth, it's not terrible at all. Children are preprogrammed to push against authority in order to establish an appropriate sense of boundaries. Having some freedom to challenge our caregivers is essential for our well-being.

Fortunately, just before most parents go over the edge, toddlers' compulsion to say no eventually subsides, at least to some extent. If handled well by the parents (i.e., if he's neither squelched nor given too much power), the child moves on to a phase of greater cooperation and desire to please. Then, somewhere in their teenage years, children have a resurgence of this need to say no, both through words and actions, as they push away from authority figures on the final stretch of growing up. They again become compelled to make a strong statement that they are unique and different.

Though we all have a need to belong, we all have an equally strong need to make our own mark in the world. If all goes well, we integrate our different characteristics into our identity, and we develop the freedom to choose what's best for us based on our unique situations. If we factor in variations in personality and temperament, this process will show up somewhat differently in each child. If we're given a lot of love and appropriate limit-setting during our youth, we become emotionally mature adults. As such, we're not afraid to take chances, but we don't impulsively put ourselves in harm's way. We feel fortified by our strengths, yet we also embrace our limitations. We're not compelled to rebel against authority just for the sake of rebelling, nor do we squelch ourselves because we're immobilized with fear. Rather, we're thoughtful about our decisions and about our responses to the needs of others.

When we receive healthy and loving boundaries from caregivers during childhood, we grow up with confidence. We feel secure enough to at times disagree with or challenge authority, specifically if we find that the demands or requests of authority figures violate our own values or goals. But we can also defer to authority if our situation so requires it. We also respect that other people may have different values than ours, and we don't get caught up in trying to get everyone to do things in our own way. We allow other people the right to assert their own selves, too. We may try to persuade and influence others toward certain values, but we ultimately recognize that we can't control others without potentially violating the rights of others. And, most importantly, if we feel threatened, we take action to keep ourselves safe.

Sounds good, doesn't it? Unfortunately, most of us didn't have the kind of childhood where the people who cared for us understood the importance of this developmental process. Even if we were lucky enough to have been raised by someone who was hip to these developmental phases, no parent can offer a perfect environment—after all, everyone has limits to their patience, and it can be very trying for an adult to handle the barrage of childhood obstinacy. As a result, most of us were raised in less-than-ideal conditions. Either we were stifled in expressing our identity no matter how much or how little we pushed on the edges, or we demonstrated such unreasonable rebelliousness that we had to be contained so as to not hurt ourselves or others. Or some of us may have been encouraged to question authority without any limits, and thereby never learned appropriate ways to accept guidance and leadership from others. Chances are a good deal of our old bruises resulted from having been unintentionally misguided through our envelope-pushing phases. Thus the connection to our problems in the workplace—many probably stem from issues or problems that arose around the formation of our identity.

Too many people enter adulthood still stuck in the terrible

twos, or in the leftover throes of teenage rebellion. Still others never pushed their limits at all, perhaps because the boundaries around them were so strict or possibly abusive that they were far too afraid. The result? We become prone to power struggles. We end up either saying "no" just to be contrary, or saying "yes" just to avoid losing favor with others. Often, the option of "maybe" doesn't even come to mind. While we continue to age chronologically, our emotional age stays much younger until we're able to master this developmental challenge.

So how do we recover from this mess? The answer: by experimenting with the whole range of available choices.

## The Power of Yes/No/Maybe

The best way to master these issues that originate in our early development is to make the commitment, at last, to grow up. While we once were entirely under the control of those who cared for us, as adults we must embrace that we have choices in terms of how we run our lives. And of course, we have to deal with the consequences of the choices we make.

Making this commitment requires that you practice responding to authority figures (or those you perceive to be in authority) on the premise that you are a full-fledged adult who has the right to make your own choices and decisions. In the workplace, you must accept that even though someone may have authority over you, they have no ultimate power over how you choose to live your life.

Once you accept this premise, then all options—yes, no, or maybe—become accessible. As I tell many of my adult patients, "We know we're really growing up when we can do what our authority figures recommend, even though they're the ones that recommended it." In other words, choosing yes, no, or maybe become conscious decisions, not just knee-jerk reactions. The coolest thing about coming to this awareness is that because you're now more attuned to your own power, you won't feel the need to impose it on other people. And you'll find that you command much more respect from others without having to demand it.

Before Paul embarked on his journey of self-improvement, he was firmly mired in this perpetual state of rebellion. If someone said "black," he'd say "white." If someone said "go," he'd say "stop." I think you get the picture. He didn't have any idea just how contrary he had become over the years. In his late twenties, Paul worked as a clerk at a law firm while he was studying for the bar exam. He was lucky that he was as smart as he was, or I'm certain he would have been fired sooner due to his obstinate behavior.

Paul argued with everyone. No matter who gave him orders, or how appropriately the orders corresponded to his job requirements, Paul would kick up a fuss. He was incapable of taking direction or accepting assignments from anyone. He always had some kind of rationale for why whatever it was would be better done his way. Sure, his ability to argue a point might later serve him well in the courtroom, but it wasn't working well at the office. If someone wanted him to do something, he didn't want to do it. If someone didn't want him to do something, he would argue as to why he should do it. In reality he was utterly clueless about what he wanted—he just simply couldn't comply with someone else's ideas.

Eventually this firm fired Paul before he ever became a lawyer. Along the way, he'd developed a pretty negative reputation around town. Ultimately, Paul came to understand that, beneath his fancy suits and confident veneer, he continued to live life as though he was a rebellious teenager. Having never gotten permission from his family to speak his mind without being ridiculed, it was as though he was making up for lost time. Fortunately, before he went too far down the path of self-destruction, Paul realized that he had to find a more effective way to express feelings that had been stifled.

Paul came to understand that following orders from his superiors didn't mean he wasn't still a man, and still in control of his life, as long as those orders didn't conflict with his core value system. He learned how to regulate his responses according to what was truly best, given his present circumstances. It took him some time, however, because Paul was one of the most stubborn clients I've ever known! But he eventually made the changes he needed to make and was able to land an associate position at a prestigious law firm.

In order to empower yourself further, try the following exercise.

### ▸ Reply Exercise

With each request made of you by an authority figure, or even by a coworker, give yourself a three-second pause. If you don't want to comply with a particular request because you think it's truly out of line, but you're prone to saying "yes" reflexively because you fear rocking the boat, then after your three-second pause try saying the following: "I think that's an interesting idea, but I'm going to have to make sure that it's something I'm okay with doing before I accept the assignment." Or you might try something even more simple, like, "Let me have a minute to think about that." Regardless of what you actually say, the idea is to interrupt your tendency to give an automatic response. In case something like this makes you nervous, remember that, in the end, you should never be hostage to your job or any of the people there. Thus, while you should certainly do what's asked of you when the request corresponds with your job description, you should never be in the position where you cave into someone else's demands, especially if they violate your code of ethics. So work hard at exercising your power to say "no" or "maybe," too.

If you're one of those people who's prone to saying "no" because you don't like being told what to do, you too need to put a buffer between a request and your response. You could say something like, "I need a little time to mull that over to make sure that I would be able to give it my best shot." Or you could try, "I know how important this is, and I don't want to make any promises I can't keep, so let me just make sure my schedule is free enough to do a good job." Then take the time to see whether it's really appropriate, or in your best interest, to comply.

Obviously you have to modify these kinds of responses according to your specific situation. What's important, however, is that you work out your resistance to doing what's asked of you. You need to experiment with saying "yes" and "maybe" more often when these responses would serve you better in your present situation. Otherwise you should consider becoming self-employed.

If you're prone to a chronic state of fence-sitting, you need to challenge yourself to make more definitive statements. As a psychologist (and recovering fence-sitter), I've often been accused of always playing both sides and never wanting to upset anyone. But while this attitude had its place as a coping mechanism before I discovered my own power to choose, I had to recognize that it didn't serve me well as an only option. My indecisiveness became so debilitating that I would even have anxiety if someone asked me what I wanted for lunch.

Challenging the fence-sitting position doesn't mean you should react impulsively. Fence-sitters, too, should use the three-second pause. But rather than giving the wishy-washy "maybe," try to commit to a "yes" or "no" if at all possible. Of course, if it's a really critical request with far-reaching job implications, then you would certainly want to exercise your delay button so that you have time to weigh the consequences of your decision. But don't let this keep you from making up your mind.

Whether you're a yes-, no-, or maybe-sayer, make sure you weigh your choices carefully on the front end so that you give yourself a better chance of following through with your decisions. However, because we can't always foresee how we're going to feel about a decision, you need to grant yourself the option of changing your mind sometimes should you discover that a choice you've made isn't really working. Remember, our goal here is to help you eliminate drama. If you force yourself to stick to a decision that you find unbearable, you're going to act out in some way (probably a dramatic way) that's liable to get you into trouble. So always strive to be thoughtful in the first place (a much easier goal, the more self-aware you are), and then make the ongoing assessments necessary to solidify your commitments.

While you're practicing your different choices along the whole yes-no-maybe continuum, keep in mind that you should be making your decisions to fit your goals. Assuming that you don't have any vindictive or ulterior motives to harm others, if you make your decisions according to your goals, you'll automatically find you have less investment in pleasing others. You'll do what's right for your career path and respect that others will take care of themselves. Most importantly, you'll realize that you won't always get what you want—but you'll have a sense of peace so that you can continue to create the positive experiences you desire and deserve.

## The Art of Constructive Leadership

By applying these tools for eliminating power struggles, you also pave the way toward becoming a more effective leader. Wherever you are in your workplace's hierarchy, it's important to understand effective leadership. Whether or not you have authority over other people doesn't matter. Creating positive relationships requires that you demonstrate a take-charge attitude in terms of your responsibilities. Because of the many different personalities we encounter in the workplace, we can't always interact with people in the same way and get the same outcomes. We have to be open to altering our interaction style to accommodate these differences. Sometimes we may need to resort to tactics that some might consider manipulative—but this doesn't have to be exploitative or negative. The way I see it, if we're trying to avoid or prevent power struggles, we need to be armed with as many alternative responses as possible.

Learning how to alter your style to fit different situations can be very effective in transcending power struggles as long as you don't become too invested in the outcome. In other words, you must still be careful to recognize where your power begins and ends. You can't *need* someone to respond a certain way. (Remember, your choices should always be about what you control, not about controlling someone else.) The goal is to expand your repertoire of behaviors in order to help you eliminate drama. Sometimes these will work, and sometimes they won't. And when they don't, you can adapt your style.

Let's consider the "back door" metaphor to illustrate what I'm saying here. You probably don't always walk through the front door of your house. Sometimes you might use the side door, or the back door, or you may even break a window if you've locked yourself out. If the goal is to get in, as long as you're not violating anyone else's rights, then it's a good idea to exhaust all possible avenues. You might decide to call a locksmith if these other methods fail. I can't imagine that anyone would simply move from their home because they couldn't get into the front door on occasion.

Constructive leadership in our workplace relationships requires being able to find all of the available ways in. The question to answer is, "What's the best method I can use to increase my chances of success?" Hence, you first need to define success, and second, assess all the possibilities of achieving it. You need to be aware of all of your resources and then use the ones that are most effective, keeping in mind that what works with one person may not work with another.

As you've learned, you can't control the effect your methods have on a situation or person. However, after getting to know our coworkers and bosses, we can usually get a pretty good sense of how they respond in different situations. As a result, we can adapt how we behave according to what are likely fairly predictable patterns. This is an important principle whether you're a boss, a manager, a coworker, or a client.

Of course, I would never recommend that you do anything that jeopardizes your integrity or that puts you or someone else in a victim position. But there's a pretty good chance that once you've healed your old bruises, you're going to learn how to see more of the options available to you, and hence a whole bunch more doors will open. As a result, you will become better at making the most out of any situation.

Craig worked for Doug, who was known for being a pretty tough cookie. Doug wasn't necessarily abusive, but he certainly had a sarcastic, impersonal way about him that required others to have a fairly thick skin when dealing with him. It could take hours of relentless persuasion and documentation to get him to listen to a point of view other than his own. Yet the people who took the time to get to know him knew that Doug could soften up if treated just the right way.

While Craig certainly didn't care much for Doug's approach to things, and at first there were times when he really wanted to quit, he eventually realized that Doug responded better to certain styles of communication than others. Craig learned that if he approached Doug with a joke or two, and some superficial banter about lightweight topics like sports, Doug was more receptive to his input. Sure, you might consider this maneuver to be a form of sucking up. But so what! No one was hurt or compromised by Craig's doing this. When he approached Doug in this way, Craig got a better outcome, and felt more listened to and respected.

Tracy ran a small café with about ten employees. She enjoyed her work and generally thought well of her crew. However, one employee, Karen, often arrived at work with a horrible attitude. Yet, once Karen got further into her day, her work shined, and she became quite personable and congenial. Tracy had the right to speak to Karen about her attitude issues, but instead she opted to work around her.

Tracy learned that if she left Karen alone for the first thirty minutes of her shift, she would eventually work herself out of her funk. Though this required Tracy to change her natural style of getting down to business, she concluded that Karen was more of an asset than a liability.

Belinda, an executive's assistant, worked for Ken, who habitually would lash out at her to the point where she felt she had no other option but to quit. But she also liked so many other things about her job—including its ample vacation time, lavish benefits, and pension—that she really didn't want to cave in and quit. She spent months tormented by what seemed to be two equally undesirable options. But through her therapy, she came to understand a third option—changing her approach to her boss.

At first, this seemed as appalling as her other options. But she gradually learned that she could actually help prevent many of Ken's temper flare-ups from getting out of hand by padding her interactions with positive reinforcement. Basically, whenever Ken would behave appropriately, she would go a bit overboard in praising him for handling a stressful situation so well. And whenever he began to show signs of losing it, she learned how to use a few very effective statements that would get her out of his line of fire. For instance, she would say, "Ken, it seems like this is very upsetting to you; I'm sure you need some time to cool off. I'll be available later so we can discuss other options." Or sometimes she might say, "Ken, I have some very pressing deadlines I absolutely have to meet on your behalf. After you get through whatever is causing you so much stress right now, we can discuss it later."

Of course, I'm not suggesting that these particular techniques will work in your situation. But I hope that they provide you with some food for thought on how to take control and become better at managing a difficult situation when you really don't feel that quitting is a desirable option.

### ▶ Visualization Exercise

Now, spend a few minutes considering some of the different ways that you could improve your workplace relationships by using these kinds of methods. Be creative in thinking up examples from your own experiences that would be fitting to your unique work situation. Keep in mind, however, that this requires really paying attention to the information you have about someone's characteristic behavior and what kinds of things seem to help them behave better. All the while, you must remember you don't have control over someone else's behavior, but you *can* improve your interactions by using all of the different interpersonal resources available to you.

# Nine

STEP SIX—

# Learn How to Tell Harmless Flirtation and Friendship from Sexual Harassment

Let me start off my thoughts on this important and very delicate subject by stating that I believe intense and romantic feelings are inevitable among adults spending hours together each day. Personal relationships are bound to happen among coworkers. And most likely, the more time we spend at work, the more likely we are to cross over interpersonal boundaries and use the workplace as an arena for socializing. I'm in no way saying that this is bad—though I do want to stress that sexual harassment is always out-of-bounds behavior—but rather that, as with all aspects of our work life, we need to be aware of the consequences of our actions and take ownership of our choices. I've included information here concerning the pros and cons of becoming a couple with someone else at work, and specifically addressed the differences between singles pairing up and married people who have affairs with coworkers. So let's start by looking at friendship and then move on up the risky-business ladder.

## Friendship

I've met some of my best friends during my years spent working at various hospital facilities. Many of my patients, friends, and acquaintances have reported that they, too, have created many lasting friendships with coworkers. After all, shared interests are built into the workplace experience, at least in terms of the work you do. Assuming you like your actual job or career, you likely have some compatibility with your coworkers. It just makes sense that if you love architecture and you work in an architectural firm, say, you're going to find others who share this passion.

Since many of us spend a great deal of our time at work, it can be quite a bonus if we can make friends while we're also accomplishing our professional goals. Hence, not only does our workplace have the potential to fulfill our needs for intellectual and creative career goals, it can also serve as a place to build lasting friendships.

While establishing friendships on the job can be very positive, these relationships can become messy if we're not careful about who we befriend and how we manage our boundaries. We must always keep in mind that we need to separate the personal from the professional. Friendships with coworkers can have negative repercussions if both parties are not in tune regarding potential issues. Exactly how these boundary issues arise in any given workplace has a lot to do with the nature of the job, status or rank in the company, level of responsibility, and the ability to keep personal issues from bleeding into professional duties.

▸ *Awareness Exercise*

To help deepen your awareness of these issues, try the following exercise. Below are three different scenarios. As you read each of them, think about potential problems that could arise. Let your mind explore all sorts of possibilities. Don't get caught up in trying to decide what's right or wrong. Instead, think of how these dilemmas might be resolved, taking into consideration what the individuals can do to reduce the chances of irreparable conflict.

1. Diana and Nancy work together in the same office. Diana doesn't have direct rank over Nancy, per se, but she definitely has seniority in the company. On occasion, the big boss asks Diana to oversee some of her

coworkers' projects. Diana and Nancy are of similar age, and they both really enjoy each other's company. They have lunch together several times per week and they often socialize together along with their partners on the weekends. One day, Nancy comes to work in tears because her boyfriend has dumped her, and she naturally expects her friend to comfort her. What are some of the issues that could arise in this type of relationship?

2. Kyle and Sue work in different departments as supervisors. Neither outranks the other. As part of company policy they've often been sent to attend professional seminars, and over the years they've become good friends. Word gets out that one department head will be chosen for a promotion. Now, they're forced to be in competition with one another. What do you think they need to do to keep their friendship intact?

3. Melody works as Bree's assistant. They've become quite close over the years as they spend a great deal of time together, and the job necessitates a lot of personal openness. Sometimes it's hard to tell who's the boss. Because Bree has grown to trust Melody with many intimate details about her life, Melody often forgets that she works under Bree. One day, Bree receives a complaint from a highly regarded employee concerning inappropriate behavior displayed by Melody. Of course, understandably, Melody expects her boss to take her side. But, because of her professionalism, Bree feels compelled to investigate the complaint just as she would with any other employee. This causes quite a rift in her relationship with Melody. Can you think of some suggestions from what you've learned thus far that could help Melody and Bree repair their relationship while at the same time preventing future conflict?

Now that you've thought about these scenarios, can you think of any similar experiences from your own work history? Once you've given this some thought, read on for my thoughts on these three situations.

Concerning Diana and Nancy, I see the biggest problem as the difference in their status, no matter how small. Diana does have some authority over Nancy, and for the two of them to pull off a successful friendship, they both have to make peace with this reality and be careful not to let this cause resentment. The other issues concern what appears to be a boundary-crossing in terms of personal matters blending into the workplace setting. It would be appropriate for Nancy to seek Diana's comfort during personal time, but that is not acceptable during company time. I see their friendship as potentially quite positive as long as each stays clear about their respective roles and status in the workplace.

Kyle and Sue will really need to work hard at staying clear about their expectations of each other. They both need to accept that they each have a right to work hard to win the promotion, and they both will have to work hard to preserve their integrity and not breach their own ethical values in pursuing this opportunity to climb the ladder. If either one resorts to any of the out-of-bounds or sabotaging behaviors discussed earlier in this book, they'll be compromising their friendship.

As for Melody and Bree, they too must be very aware of each other's status and their roles. Melody, especially, needs to work through her belief that she deserves special treatment simply because she's Bree's trusted right hand. Bree needs to be able to follow protocol and ensure that she does not treat Melody differently than other employees in the same situation. If others in their workplace were to perceive any favoritism, it could seriously affect the whole group's morale. Because of their significant difference in power and status, they need to be particularly cautious about keeping their friendship separate from the workplace. Not an easy task, but doable if both agree to respect their differences in power and thereby apply appropriate expectations.

As you can see, in all of these scenarios there needs to be a clear distinction between the professional relationship and the friendship. When these get blurred, it can lead to trouble. I've known many people who've messed up their careers because they try to befriend everyone and not keep clear boundaries. In my experience, the more disparate the rank or status between coworkers, the trickier and potentially messier the situation if the workers attempt to maintain a friendship. It's not impossible, but it definitely requires a strong mutual commitment to staying psychologically and emotionally healthy.

## Flirtation

Sexuality is an integral part of human life, and we can't ignore that we may at times experience strong chemistry with someone else at work. This is simply a reality of adult life. Though we can make choices about whether we act on our impulses, we cannot deny those impulses' potential to surface. So please refrain from shaming yourself if you have had an attraction to someone with whom you work.

Though flirting in the workplace is often thought of as taboo, I think it's very important to understand the distinction between flirtation and sexual harassment—which, again, is never okay! Flirtation can be distinguished from sexual harassment in many ways:

- Flirting, on the most basic level, tends to feel good, whereas being the target of harassment feels bad.
- Flirting is consensual and generally based on perceived mutual attraction.
- Flirting is often subtle, and usually inexplicit.
- Flirtation tends to be complimentary and reciprocal. It becomes harassment if one of the participants no longer wishes to "play" and the other continues anyway.
- Flirting does not involve attempts to control one another through manipulation or blackmail.
- Flirtation is never accompanied by any threats of job loss, demotion, or any other consequence that would threaten the job security of those involved in the flirting.

Understanding that sexual tension exists and that chemistry doesn't constitute harassment does not answer the question of whether it's okay to flirt at work. In fact, the appropriateness of flirtation in a workplace environment continues to be debatable. It's not against the law, nor is anyone necessarily considered a "victim" if they participate in a mutual flirtation, as is the case with sexual harassment. But it's not without its own potential dangers. In fact, anyone who engages in flirting dives down a slippery slope. Though there may not be any legal repercussions to flirting, as there surely can be with harassment, you are taking a risk that someone you flirt with may become offended or may come to *perceive* your behavior as harassment. What might begin as innocent flirtation may escalate to a level that one of the participants feels is invasive or no longer within acceptable bounds.

Even if you've always been successful at reading other people's attraction to you, you're still taking a pretty big risk if you act on an attraction you perceive from someone else at work and then turn out to be wrong. Because you have no control over how someone else will interpret your behavior, you might even incorrectly believe that your behavior is okay when it's actually being perceived as unwanted or even threatening. You might misperceive someone's reaction as welcoming and equally flirtatious when, in fact, the recipient may simply not know how to discourage you.

Another concern, if you're a confirmed flirter, is the question of your flirtee. Is this person single and unattached, or married? For that matter, are *you* single or married? Many people subscribe to the belief that flirting is harmless. While this may be true in many circumstances, it can and does often lead to problems. For instance, what if a flirter is in an intimate relationship with someone who isn't the object of the flirtation? Is this appropriate behavior?

Many might argue that what your partner doesn't know won't hurt him. But I beg to differ. Anytime we take an expression of our sexual energy, even in a mild form like flirting, and direct it toward someone who isn't our mate, we are subtly breaching trust and potentially creating distance in our primary intimate relationship. Flirting is also used by some as a distraction from confronting problems in a primary relationship. In these kinds of situations, all sorts of problems can ensue, either from the unaddressed problems or from a flirtation that grows into something more. Also, what if the person you flirt with takes offense that you are married or attached to someone else? What do your actions say about you in that situation? Could this cost you respect in the workplace? I think it's always in our best interest to consider these questions and potential consequences very carefully before we choose to cross from friendly behavior to flirting behavior.

Take care to distinguish flirting from friendly behavior, even though they can look very much alike. Close attention to nonverbal cues (such as tone of voice, inflections, length of eye contact, and body language) will make the differences more apparent. Mostly these differences concern motivation. When someone is flirting, they're conveying a sense of attraction. If you're just being friendly, you're simply conveying pleasant or positive energy.

### ▶ Flirtation Exercise

Just for fun, take a moment and think of how many different ways you could say to a coworker, "Hey, your smile really brightens up my day!" Experiment with your body language and tone of voice. Try saying it as a compliment or as an invitation to get to know you better. If you have a friend you can do this with, all the better. Mind you, this is a game to play outside the workplace to give you a safe way to discover the variety of ways a particular gesture or expression could be interpreted. Have a friend try to guess whether you're trying to be flirty or simply friendly.

As you've probably already learned by now, I try to discourage thinking about these kinds of issues as absolutes—that is, as "right" or "wrong"—since there are so many gray areas. I think it's far more helpful to think in terms of the potential consequences of your behavior. It's helpful to ask yourself whether you can handle whatever those consequences might be. That way, you eliminate the likelihood that you'll end up feeling like a victim. For instance, if your company frowns upon flirting in the workplace, but you're really attracted to some guy who you think might feel the same about you, you might choose to test the waters. But if so, you shouldn't be surprised if your behavior gets you a reprimand.

## Flirting Don'ts

I try to refrain from judgment for the most part, but I have no qualms about making emphatic statements against something if it has the potential to harm another person, as is the case in sexual harassment. Also, concerning flirting, I think there are a couple of scenarios that would absolutely constitute out-of-bounds behavior. Below is a list of conditions under which I would strongly discourage acting on any temptation toward workplace flirting:

- Those engaged in the flirting are of *unequal* status, such as if one is a subordinate, the other is the boss. If you're the boss and you try to flirt with someone over whom you have power, or even just someone you outrank, you could be perceived as sexually harassing, even if the flirtation appears welcome or is reciprocated. On the flip side, even if you're flirting upward (i.e., toward a coworker or boss who has rank or power over you), you run the risk of appearing to be a troublemaker. Plus, if you were to end up in a situation where you took the flirting to another step (i.e., engaged in some kind of romance) and you ended up regretting it, or even feeling as though you were taken advantage of, you would not be taken very seriously should you wish to pursue a case of harassment.
- Your place of employment has well-defined policies against flirting in the workplace. This doesn't mean that you can't flirt. Just be smart—take it outside the office. (But keep in mind all the potential risks of flirting with a coworker.)
- You're not that good at interpreting signals. Let's face it: we're not all skilled at the same things. Some people

just aren't that great at picking up on when someone is being flirty versus when they're just being friendly. If this describes you, then you have an added risk if you flirt. Hey, even those who are pretty good at reading these signals can make mistakes. It's even riskier when you're not sophisticated in this area. Don't be ashamed. There's nothing wrong with you. If you want to improve your flirting skills, by all means, go out and get help. Just keep it out of the workplace.

Don't forget the importance of context when it comes to flirting. For instance, if you work for a large company as a sales representative where you rarely interact with office staff and you happen to see someone at an annual meeting and you decide to flirt with him, there's probably not going to be much of an issue. But flirting with someone you're required to interact with daily increases your risks of negative fallout.

Flirting can be a very normal and healthy means for letting people know you're interested in them. But—as with all of our other behaviors—we need to be responsible for the effects our behavior choices may have on how others perceive us. So whatever you do, first be informed of your company's policy; second, be aware of how others perceive how you behave; and third, don't succumb to a victim mentality if you decide to engage in this potentially risky behavior.

## Office Romance

Though many companies not only frown on office romance, but even have specific policies forbidding it, there's no law against being attracted to, or even falling in love with, someone in your workplace. Of course, it's reasonable for companies to assert policies against displaying certain behaviors in the workplace setting, but employers don't have the right to dictate what you do in your personal life. If you fall in love with or start dating someone in your office, I simply suggest that you don't screw yourself by breaking the code at your job. And as with flirting, stay conscious and mindful about your decisions and their potential risks. Otherwise the potential risks can be significantly greater, with hugely more devastating emotional and professional repercussions than those associated with simply flirting.

If you choose to date or get serious with someone whom you've met in the workplace, make sure that you are very clear about what you each expect from the other should things not work out. And be aware that even after some frank and forthright discussions in this vein, you can't always predict how people will behave or feel if their hearts get broken. This goes for you too, of course. Be sure to resolve in your own mind that you might have to forsake your job should you get involved with someone from your workplace and it ends up not working out for one or both of you, keeping in mind that the more closely you work with someone, the harder and potentially more painful it can be to carry on should there be a parting of ways. But, again, this is not a judgment or a proscription against dating a coworker, just an important note of caution.

While there are certainly some risks to two single coworkers dating, these pale in comparison to the potential dangers of getting involved in an extramarital situation. While many people justify and rationalize having a fling or affair, I would suggest that you check in with your conscience before you get into this kind of situation. Not only do you have to answer to your own conscience, but think carefully about how you would feel if your mate found out. Or think about what would happen if someone in the office became aware of what was happening. You can rarely, if ever, recover once you've lost the trust or respect of your peers.

Of course, the most risky and inappropriate romantic scenario is that between superior and subordinate. Though the heat of the moment may compel people to lose sight of the differences in power, beware if the excitement wears off or turns sour. If you're the boss, you might have just landed yourself a lawsuit charging you with sexual harassment, no matter how mutual the attraction may have been. Plus, you could be accused of sexual harassment by anyone in the company should someone perceive you as misusing your power.

## Sexual Harassment

What follows here is a guideline aimed at providing a general framework for thinking about sexual harassment. It's designed for you to use in examining your own situation. What it's not is a strict legal definition. If you believe that you've been a victim of sexual harassment, the information I present here will not suffice. Please seek legal counsel immediately, before taking any action, so that you can find out what you need to know about your rights under the law and how to pursue the best course of action.

Though women are the most frequent targets of sexual harassment, and most harassers are male, men can be victims too and therefore should not be excluded when addressing this topic. There are many different definitions of sexual harassment, which can be found in different organizations' official policies and in local and federal statutes. But the essence of harassment is that it involves sexual behavior or expressions—which could be as simple as comments, gestures, or even just the posting of pictures or other images, right up through more direct sexual suggestions or advances, all the way to outright demands for sexual acts—that are not welcomed by the people to whom these expressions are directed. If submission to or acceptance of these kinds of sexual expressions is necessary—whether explicitly or implicitly—in order for people to perform their jobs, or even to keep their jobs, then those people have been subject to sexual harassment.

In a harassment situation, one person is the harasser and another is the target of the harassment. One of the keys to understanding what constitutes harassment is whether the sexual expressions are perceived as unwelcome by the person who is harassed, as opposed to the harasser. To qualify as harassment, the sexual expressions must be perceived as intimidating, interfering, or used as a threat against the target's livelihood at work. This is important because it reduces the chances of false accusations. Since sexual harassment is a serious crime, it would be awful for someone to be accused of harassment if the accuser herself had encouraged any sexual expressions during an interaction with the accused harasser. At the same time, it highlights that no one should ever have to be subjected to sexual advances or insinuations that are unwelcome.

Though there's no clear-cut profile of the sexual harasser, most of those who engage in this behavior closely resemble the psychological profile associated with bullies. Harassers tend to:

- Be aggressive and domineering
- Use harassment as a way to feel powerful or to intimidate others
- Use their actions as a way to hide from feelings of inadequacy, jealousy, envy, or low self-esteem
- Have a fundamental disregard for the rights of others
- Be narcissistic (highly self-absorbed), void of the ability to empathize with others
- Feel entitled to behave as they do without consequences
- Have a history of serial harassment—i.e., their behavior is not situation-specific, but rather a pattern.

Some sexual harassers may have been abused in their childhood, but even people who've been victimized this way should still be accountable for their behavior as adults. Harassment is a behavior. And behaviors are something we all have choices about. Hence, there is no legitimate reason for someone to harass another.

When suspected, or even when fully busted, sexual harassers notoriously manipulate others into believing that either they didn't know what they were doing or that the victim came onto them, thereby leaving them no choice. They will almost always lie and distort the situation to their own advantage. They try to deceive others into believing that they are victims too and should be treated with leniency.

Unfortunately, probably due to ignorance or fear, many people continue to uphold myths about those who are targets of harassment. They may believe that victims "ask for" or invite the harassment. They may think that victims are weak or overly sensitive. Or they may view victims as sharing equal responsibility with their harassers, thereby denying that there even is a victim in a harassment situation.

Victims who actually take a stance against their harassment (e.g., by suing the harasser and/or their employer) are often accused of being "money-hungry" or as attempting to cover-up their own involvement in sexual banter or other exchanges in order to avoid embarrassment. As frequently happens in rape cases, those who defend a perpetrator or who minimize the seriousness of the offense will often try to bring up anything negative they can about the alleged victim's character in order to cast doubt on the victim's credibility.

While today there is a great deal more awareness and understanding of sexual harassment, many companies continue to resist dealing with it. I've even worked with some people who were fired for "making waves" because they outed a harasser. Of course, these employers had to find clever ways to disguise the real reason behind the termination. And, while there have always been occasions where an alleged victim has made up a story for personal gain, as we say, "one bad apple shouldn't spoil the whole bunch." Just because a few people may have tried to pull off scams doesn't mean that harassment doesn't exist. Real cases of harassment deserve attention!

So what are you supposed to do if you've been the target of harassment?

Below are some tips:

- Find out your company's policy on sexual harassment and protocol for action, and follow that protocol.
- Seek legal advice. Many attorneys will provide a free twenty- to thirty-minute consultation over the telephone to provide you with basic information.
- Use the internet to find agencies aimed to help harassment victims.
- Take good care of yourself mentally, spiritually, and physically—you'll need all the energy you can get to make it through this experience.
- Use the tools in this book for self-love and nurturance.
- Don't blame yourself.

- Take a course in sexual harassment prevention.
- Encourage your company to provide sexual harassment awareness and prevention training.
- If your company won't take action against a harasser, or if you fear the repercussions of pursuing a case, seek other employment. No matter how cushy your job, how great the benefits, or whatever else keeps you there, nothing can ever be worth selling out your right to be treated fairly.

Please also keep in mind that while no one should ever have the right to violate another person, you must always be responsible for practicing good self-care in order to minimize your chances of being victimized. Please do not confuse this with "blaming the victim." As you've learned, we aren't responsible for other people's behavior, good or bad. But we *are* responsible for the bad situations we choose to keep ourselves in. And we are also responsible for doing the best we can to prevent ourselves from being harmed.

Consider Jessica's situation. At her workplace, Jessica encountered the classic office creep. He leered at her and would often make what sounded to her like barking noises under his breath as he walked by her in the hall. His behavior was clearly inappropriate but never obvious to anyone else around her. His mere presence caused her anxiety and disrupted her concentration and performance.

Jessica was afraid to inform her boss. She didn't think she would be taken seriously. While her boss wasn't as much of a cad as this guy, he seemed to subscribe to the "old boys' club" mentality, where women's primary purpose on earth was to serve men's arousal needs. (Without being more graphic, I think you get the picture.) Jessica liked the independence of her job and figured she'd encounter this kind of thing anywhere she went, in that she worked in a male-dominated profession. Thus, she talked herself out of taking charge of her situation. Unfortunately, because of her low self-esteem and faulty beliefs about her rights, Jessica stayed in this destructive environment way too long.

After a few months of therapy, during which she gained a much better grasp of what it meant to support her own well-being, Jessica finally stood up to the mistreatment and asked her boss to do something about it. Fortunately for Jessica, her boss was attuned enough to the risk of a potential lawsuit that he reprimanded the harasser and moved him to another department. While this made the situation better in the short run, Jessica eventually concluded that she didn't want to work in a company that wouldn't really go to bat for employees who were being harassed.

Jessica also learned that, while she was in no way responsible for being harassed, she could have taken better care of herself along the way—especially while she was trying to decide how best to approach her challenging situation. Not that she should have altered how she reacted to someone else's out-of-bounds behavior, but sometimes we do need to do certain things to protect ourselves. For instance, she could have made a statement—out loud, directly to the harasser—that his behavior would not be tolerated. Or she could have made sure that she kept out of his way. In the end, of course, her best choice was to move on.

One of the most difficult decisions concerning sexual harassment is whether to pursue legal prosecution. Many people feel intimidated by the legal system, or they fear the stigma associated with being involved in a harassment case. Others fear backlash and further victimization. Of course, if you work for a company that has a zero-tolerance policy for sexual harassment, it can certainly help matters, but even then going through the legal system can be enormously taxing. This is not to say that one shouldn't take action. Quite the contrary. But I think it's helpful to have a good idea what you're going to be up against in order to increase your odds of weathering the storm.

If you were ever faced with this dilemma, or should you ever be in this situation, keep in mind the following:

- You are not a perpetrator if you hold someone accountable for their inappropriate actions. As an example, should you ever witness a crime, you are doing nothing wrong by turning in the criminal. In the case of harassment, if you are a victim, you are doing nothing wrong by naming your harasser and holding him (or her) accountable.

- Don't blame yourself for being a target—but do make any changes necessary to better your chances of keeping safe in the future. Just as you would never put a child in a class-room with a known sexual offender, try never to put your-self in positions where you know there could be trouble.
- Boost your emotional well-being by educating yourself and joining a support group.
- Weigh all the pros and cons of how to pursue your case, making sure to account for your personality, stamina, and tolerance for heavy-duty confrontation.
- Get help distinguishing real danger from imagined danger. If the only reason you wouldn't pursue a case is because you fear the process, see whether you can work through your fears and then decide what to do.
- Don't let anyone else pressure you into making a deci-sion. You're the one who has to live with yourself. No one else can make these choices for you.

Most importantly, I hope that you will never have to encounter such a scenario. But if you have already, or if you are currently caught up in a sexual harassment case, be good to yourself and keep living life fully during the process. The best outcome will ensue when you don't give away your power over yourself and your choices. Take charge of your life with strength and conviction. Through my more then twenty years of clinical practice, I've seen time and time again that the healthier we become emotionally, the less often we end up in situations where we will be victimized. And even if we do get trapped, those difficulties are short-lived because we make choices on behalf of our desire to thrive.

▶ *Relaxation Exercise*

Before moving to another chapter, I suggest you to take a break. This chapter has given you a lot to think about. If you've been sitting and reading for a while, stand up and stretch. Breathe deeply and let go of any pent-up tension. We've hit on some pretty heavy topics, and I've asked a lot of you. You've been thinking, writing, contemplating, and changing attitudes and behaviors. Of course, it's always a good idea to keep revisiting the concepts and exercises spread throughout all of the chapters, but you need to also make space to relax and enjoy the fruits of your hard work. So take a few minutes at least to clear your head and open up to even more challenges.

# Ten

STEP SEVEN—
# Develop a Sense of Humor Toward Inevitable Workplace Turmoil

Too many workplace environments resemble a soap opera set. Drama abounds, and no matter how much you work on bettering yourself, you're inevitably going to be confronted with others' dysfunctional behavior over the course of your work life. After all, not everyone has made the commitment toward personal development that you have. Very few people out of the entire population actually care about understanding the psychology behind developing positive relationships, let alone are willing to do the work necessary to change their negative patterns.

Many people go through their whole lives stuck in familiar patterns of behavior and thinking, no matter how unhappy those patterns make them. They won't take any steps to change, no matter what. You, however, are making important strides toward bettering your own situation and getting the best you possibly can from your workplace environment. And once again, you deserve applause for those efforts!

Just because few others may do what's necessary to improve their own situations doesn't mean your efforts are wasted. Quite the contrary. Because you're now well aware that even though you can't make other people change, you can change your own perspective on what you expect of others. You no longer have to become so frustrated and disappointed when others don't rise to the level you're trying to achieve. Instead, you can accept this reality and make the best of it. You can make light and laugh about it. Most importantly, you can also learn to laugh at yourself—not in a shaming way, but in a playful, endearing way.

As with all new adventures we take, we have to be patient and accept that we may not achieve mastery over our goals as quickly as we identify them. But we can certainly speed growth by fertilizing the field. In terms of lightening up in the workplace, we can put two very important practices into motion right away: 1) applying the art of stress reduction, and 2) accepting the reality that there are very few crises in life. By deploying these two principles, you further minimize the power you give away to others by allowing them to affect your mood. And then you won't have to take the drama so seriously.

## Stress Reduction

There's no way you can be lighthearted and stressed at the same time. These are two mutually exclusive states of being. But to be able to laugh, you simply must create the space to do so.

Too often, people get caught up in surrounding drama, and they lose sight of how important it is to separate and take a break. But, unless you carve out the time and space from your schedule to calm yourself down, you're headed for a life of chronic anxiety. While you can't really change your genetic blueprint, you do have a great deal of influence over your own physical and mental well-being based on (you guessed it) the choices you make. So get out those meditation tapes, light some candles, and have a lounge in the tub. Or take a class or two specifically aimed at reducing stress, such as yoga, meditation, pottery, or whatever other activity you find soothing.

I recommend to my patients that they practice some form of stress-reducing activity at least twice per day for a minimum of fifteen-minute intervals. Find an outlet that works for you. Keep in mind that what reduces stress in one person may actually increase tension in another. Therefore, I can't give you a specific formula. You need to be creative, and you need to listen to your body's signals, and then take it from there.

Also, sometimes we might find that a particular method works for a while and then seems to lose its relaxation effect. If this happens, don't jump ship. Instead, try out some different techniques. For instance, I used to go on long jogs to relieve my stress. But, no big surprise, my knees have become cranky and uncooperative as I've gotten older. Thus, what used to give me great pleasure now sometimes feels more like a chore. So I've had to find other sources of exercise. While I continue to see the benefit of keeping my body in motion, I've also discovered that I really needed to build in some comforting and soothing activities to get a true sense of relaxation. I had to learn ways to help my body *rest*. I had to get myself to take a deep breath, stand still for a moment, and really enjoy the coffee—decaf, that is, or my heart starts to race!

Thus far, I've only highlighted physical means to reduce stress, but we can also rid our tension through psychological tools—i.e., by changing how we think about the world and how we process information. What follows is a list of psychological tools for stress reduction:

1. Monitor how you talk about (and to) yourself. We can't possibly experience inner peace if we're harping on ourselves, saying demeaning things, or criticizing our every move. That doesn't mean we should stop evaluating the effectiveness of our behavior, but we should keep tabs on ourselves with curiosity, patience, understanding, and kindness. Otherwise, we'll set in motion a shame spiral and kick into gear those defenses that ultimately keep us from fully experiencing life. So put down the hammer, and put on a smile.

2. Start each day with a positive affirmation. Say something inspiring to keep you motivated toward positive change. Repeat your mantra at intervals throughout the day. For instance, you might start your morning with a big stretch and the words, "I'm going to make the most of every situation I encounter today." Or, "Today's another day for an opportunity to learn something new."

3. End each day by praising yourself for taking positive action. When you return home from work, give yourself a big pat on the back. Say something like, "Good job for making an effort today," or whatever words feel good to you. If you feel that you fell off your growth path, try to figure out why. What buttons got pushed? Did you forget your mission of staying positive? What would help you do better tomorrow? Answering these questions should help you get back on track. But make sure to ask yourself these questions with curiosity, and not with judgment or ridicule.

4. Set realistic goals. You know yourself pretty well—or at least you're involved in the process of self-discovery. So don't set yourself up to fail by expecting to move mountains in a day. You're only human. The more you stay in the present moment, accepting the power and choices you have, the more successful you'll be.

5. Don't put off to tomorrow what you can do today, as long as you work, rest, and play in balanced fashion. Have you ever gone to the movies on your day off and couldn't really enjoy it because you felt like you were supposed to be doing something else? Or have you ever been at work, unable to concentrate because your friends or loved ones have been complaining that you're never around for them anymore? Or maybe you've been hiding under the covers feeling tense, not wanting to get up but recognizing that you've been trying to sleep away all your woes?

All of these would signal that you're overstretched in some areas and understretched in others. While we may not always be able to devote a balanced amount of time toward rest, work, and play, we need to come pretty close over the long run. If you spend months at a time working extra-long hours, you're going to pay a high price in stress. Your body needs to rest, and your spirit needs time to play. Otherwise, you'll lose your ability to laugh. So make sure you realign and rebalance your priorities.

6. Don't look too far forward and don't look too far back. Keep your focus on the present and try to live each moment fully. I know, you have bills to pay, appointments to keep, kids to get to school, a husband who wants dinner, and a multitude of other obligations. There's always something pending. But when was the last time that *worrying* about something got the task done? Again, place your focus where you have the power, which is in the present moment. It's certainly okay to have dreams and fantasies—these don't cause stress. It's the worrying about the future, or even the past (a time zone in which we have zero power), that gets us into trouble. Get rid of worry and take action instead.

7. Be realistic about the limitations of others. No one's perfect. As you've learned, everyone has at least some old stuff that can get the best of them. But I recommend that as long as someone isn't operating out of bounds or routinely wreaking havoc in your life, cut him or her some slack. Haven't you had a bad day or two where you haven't been the nicest person to be around? Try practicing some compassion and empathy toward someone else who seems to be having a bad day.

8. Stop catastrophizing—that is, always fearing the worst even when there's no sign of imminent disaster. Clearly, if you were abused or have lived through multiple traumas in your life, you're not going to give up this tendency very easily. And, of course, sometimes true disaster does strike. But so often we have no control over these events, yet we waste mental energy on the illusion that if we ponder every possibility, maybe we can prevent the catastrophe.

   In my work, I've heard thousands of descriptions of pending doom: "If I get fired, I'll never work again." "If I don't meet that deadline, no one at the office will ever forgive me." "I just know that I'll never be good enough to get that promotion." These are just a few of the projected workplace catastrophes that I've heard. Far more often than not, however, these anticipated events never happen. Or if they do, the person who feared them may be even worse off because she's exhausted all her energy worrying instead of building the resources she needed to handle whatever comes her way.

For instance, where I live in Southern California, we have lots of earthquakes, some very large and quite disastrous. But most of us residents don't possess psychic abilities and thus can't predict when these are going to hit. What we can do, however, is set up our cars, homes, and offices with earthquake preparedness kits and learn all we can about how to keep ourselves as safe as possible should an earthquake occur. We could spend every day living as though the "big one" is about to hit, but what if it doesn't? Then we've wasted precious time that could have been spent enjoying our lives.

Of course, having been a most polished catastrophizer myself, I know how hard it can be to turn off these thoughts once they've taken over. But assuming that you're not afflicted with a biochemical imbalance, which could be contributing to creating obsessive thoughts, you should be able to put a wedge in this thinking by applying the stress-reduction tools I've suggested here.

You can also try replacing these thoughts with more soothing ones whenever they arise. For instance, if you worry constantly about getting fired, start by assessing the likelihood of this happening. Assuming that this is really just a worry you've manufactured in your own mind, then when you feel this fear arise, say something like, "I understand that I would be afraid of getting axed because I do have a tendency to worry about things. But for now, since there's no evidence to support this fear,

I'm going to put my energy into what I have control over right now, which is to do a good job."

9. Spend time with friends and loved ones who are comfortable offering you support. Sometimes we can get pretty tapped out from everything we do day in and day out. While it's really important to be able to self-soothe, it certainly won't hurt to have others who can provide us with backup to help regenerate our energy. Ask them for a hug or for time to talk about your concerns. If you don't have this kind of support network, it's worth spending some of your energy building one. Otherwise, you'll be more likely to seek the wrong people to get your needs met. Remember, our bosses and coworkers shouldn't be expected to nurture our emotional needs.

10. Practice belly laughing. If you want to laugh more, you have to laugh in the first place. Start with a smile and then think of something funny. Buy or borrow a couple of humor books if you can't think of anything. When you begin laughing, deepen it. Don't be shy! Laughing is contagious.

    If you have kids (or even a group of friends who love to act like kids), play the following game. Everyone lies down in a circle, each with their head on their neighbor's stomach. One person starts to laugh and then, ideally this creates a chain event of laughing around the circle. Oh, come on! Give it a try.

Except for numbers 9 and 10, you can use any of these tools throughout your workday as well as on your time off. (Though it would be pretty funny to imagine your most uptight coworkers practicing the belly-laugh exercise on their lunch hour! Yeah, go ahead, imagine it—just don't suggest it at your next staff meeting.) Anytime you're feeling stressed, try picking a tool from the list and putting it into practice.

## Where's the Fire?

Have you ever laughed while watching a news report showing a horrific scene of people being rescued in a fire? I doubt it. No crisis, disaster, or true catastrophe is funny. But how many times during your workday have you perceived a situation or interaction to be of crisis magnitude only to look back after it's been resolved and think, "What a waste of time; that wasn't a big deal at all"?

In order to be able to kick back and laugh a little (or a lot, if you can), you have to work on truly distinguishing real danger from imagined danger. Ask yourself, "What's the worst thing that can happen if whatever I'm worried about were to come true?" If the answer isn't death or physical harm, it's probably not a true crisis. You can use all the tools throughout this book to get you through. Remember, once you're an adult, you're rarely ever a victim, particularly in the workplace. You always have choices over your destiny.

For myself, I'll never forget (though now I can remember without emotional pain) how often I've been told not to make mountains out of molehills. I hated hearing this phrase. I couldn't help it—I always took things very seriously, especially when I was a child. While I wish I had received more compassion for my sensitivity during my childhood, I've come to realize that I allowed this tendency to carry on far too long into my adulthood. I can't tell you how many times I was told to lighten up. Now I think, "If only I had listened sooner." I've certainly come to appreciate that there is often great merit to these little sayings. It's really true: I don't have to make mountains out of molehills, and I can lighten up!

So without shaming yourself, take this to heart as a way to enjoy more humor and experience less stress and emotional pain. Don't take the behavior of others quite so seriously unless they're really crossing the line.

▶ *Calming Visualization*

Picture yourself as a firefighter fully loaded with protective gear and a powerful water hose. Anytime you feel as though a coworker or boss is getting the best of you and your tools for self-soothing aren't working, imagine you can turn on the water to whatever pressure the fire requires and squirt away. I hope this image will give you the strength you need to deal with the situation or inter-action at hand.

If this image doesn't work for you, try picturing the person who's getting under your skin as a cartoon character with a really squeaky voice. And if neither of these serves to help you regain your sense of power, go ahead and be creative—make one up that boosts your inner strength.

Of course, I caution you to practice these images only if they help you calm down—and if they don't make the situation worse. In other words, don't put yourself in the position where you're laughing at someone who's trying to be serious and getting your-self in trouble. While you may not always be able to apply this technique in the heat of the moment, you can always entertain these fantasies on your break time or after work.

So come on—laugh a little!

# Eleven

# Handling Special Circumstances— Such As, What If Your Boss Really *Is* Your Mother?

Hey, lots of people work with one or more family members. This doesn't have to be a problem as long as the family connection doesn't interfere with workplace performance. But if you work with or for someone who once legitimately had authority over you during your childhood, you need to be especially careful to maintain your adult sense of yourself in the workplace. Since there would likely be more emotional attachment among relatives, this circumstance can pose additional pressures and render you a very easy target for the transference bug. But don't despair! Unless you're under legal age, or completely dependent on the relative for your livelihood and/or financial survival, everything in this book still applies—with a few additional twists.

Generally, if we feel any love at all for this family member, we're usually more timid about hurting her feelings than we would be with an unrelated coworker. And harming or losing a working relationship with a family member is much more painful and problematic than it would be with any other coworker. Plus, we may also have a greater need for approval or admiration from family members.

Since the interpersonal stakes are higher when working with loved ones, we need to be especially conscientious about being professional and not allowing our personal needs to get in the way of good judgment. At the same time, we need to be careful not to hold ourselves hostage to a situation simply because our boss is a parent or other relative. It's a good idea to work through any unfinished business (you know, those old emotional bruises) before undertaking a professional relationship with a family member, though of course this isn't always possible. At the very least, it's important to be aware of your issues should you engage in the family business.

Paul's father, Joe, managed the books for Paul's small business. This should have been a great way for Paul to cut down on costs. But as it turned out, Joe continually meddled in Paul's personal affairs and often caused rifts between Paul and Lori, Paul's wife. Lori wished that Paul would set better boundaries with his dad, or else kick him out of the business. However, Paul feared upsetting his dad and losing favor with him. Unfortunately, this story didn't have a happy ending. Paul refused to tackle this conflict, putting his dad's feelings first, and Lori and Paul divorced.

Though it's impossible to predict how the story might have ended had Paul made different choices, Paul eventually came to understand that he might have been able to save his marriage had he handled his dad differently. He eventually recognized that he could let his dad know how much he cared about him without giving him so much involvement in managing his life. Paul needed to establish more of an adult-to-adult relationship with his dad. Fortunately, he began taking steps in this direction. While Joe has become pretty angry and hurt at times, Paul has stuck to his guns, and Joe has started to come around to seeing the need for the separation.

Talia and Mariah, two sisters, had a far more positive experience working together. They owned and operated a small business they had inherited following their father's death. At first, they wrestled with many power struggles. Mariah, being three years older, initially took on the role of "bossy big sister," as she had in their childhood. And unbeknownst to both of them, Talia inadvertently set herself up for this by sending subtle signals that she was less competent than Mariah to make business decisions.

Through hard work and open dialogue concerning what each of them was doing to create this toxic dynamic, both sisters were able to change their own behavior in ways that eliminated the old significance of their age difference. After all, while three years represents a pretty big developmental difference between preteens, or even teenagers, it doesn't represent much difference for women in their thirties, at least not in terms of ability to do payroll or schedule employees. While Mariah was certainly more accomplished at certain aspects of the business than Talia (and vice versa), this had nothing to do with Mariah being the older sister. Rather, their differences were attributable to their separate interests and experiences. By coming to respect that each of them had strengths they brought to the business, neither felt the need to compete for higher rank or for more authority.

Of course, Mariah and Talia present a somewhat unique situation in that both of them were highly motivated to look at their own part in causing their troubles. More often than not, my experience has taught me that family members pull for maintaining the status quo—that is, unconsciously seeking to keep their traditional dysfunction active. In fact, if one member tries to pull out of the pattern, the others will fight even harder to restore the original balance, no matter how toxic. So don't be surprised if you encounter a great deal of resistance should you attempt to enlist a family member who is your boss or coworker into a process of change. Again, I'm not pointing this out to convey that it's wrong to work with family. I just want you to be especially sensitive to the issues that may arise.

If working with a relative has led you into problems that seem insurmountable, I highly recommend that you seek at least a couple of counseling sessions—ideally, if possible, joint sessions with the family member in question. Without a doubt, these situations can be very delicate, and a third party can help you decide how to address problems without making them worse. As a general rule, however, I recommend refraining from mixing family with business if possible, unless you have a rock-solid relationship, with similar values and visions from the get-go.

## Gender Dynamics

So many permutations and combinations exist when it comes to gender dynamics in the workplace—for instance: male-male coworkers, male coworker with male boss, male-female coworkers, male employee with female boss, female employee with male boss, female-female coworkers, and female employee with female boss. Of course, defining all the potential dynamics among these different combinations could fill an entire book, without even mentioning what happens when a team of male-dominant employees contend with a female boss, or a group of female-dominant coworkers have to relate to a male boss, or any other potential groupings.

Rather than detail all these possibilities, I've outlined below some highlights of three general pairings: men with men, women with women, and men with women, regardless of rank. Please understand that, as in earlier chapters of this book, the descriptions I supply here may not necessarily fit your experience. Many people and many workplaces may have evolved beyond these dynamics. Plus, these are generic, almost stereotypical statements that don't specifically account for one's unique unhealed childhood issues. So please review these descriptions simply as a means to provoke thought about whether any of this kind of stuff might be at play in your workplace. I'm fully aware that I might have my own biases operating here; you might notice completely different trends at your workplace, or none at all. Also, these descriptions are not based on any scientific research, but rather my years of practice and other sources of professional experience.

## Men with Men

Men tend to be more okay with overt expressions of competition. By this I mean that they don't necessarily feel particularly stressed by competitive energy. Of course this isn't the case with all men, but it's a trend I've noticed. It makes sense, since boys are taught very early on that competition is a good thing—i.e., that it's part of human nature to be competitive. Thus, many men have an easy time adjusting to the competitive aspect of the workplace. It's a familiar state of affairs, and perceived as a normal and healthy part of the workplace environment. Many men even thrive on this energy and express a loss of motivation in more cooperative environments.

Men also often communicate their feelings through back-and-forth banter or with teasing and joke-telling. And they tend to shy away from direct conversations surrounding feelings. Many tend to relate to other people with a more task-oriented perspective, and pay less attention to interpersonal process. Men are often perceived as being more concerned with material success than their female counterparts, as indicated by the more aggressive way they seek promotions and raises. I've also noticed that men I know tend to speak less about the quality of their workplace relationships than do women.

However, while some men may not feel comfortable talking about the quality of their interactions as openly as women do, many are in fact quite bothered when they perceive that they're not getting along well with others or that they're not well-liked. Do you see these trends in your workplace, or do you see different patterns?

## Women with Women

We women have gained the reputation of being more catty and manipulative than men, and more likely to express our aggression and competitiveness in indirect ways. We're often thought of as too "emotional," and may be more likely to expect that our efforts and feelings should matter as much as our actual work performance. We seem to admit (outwardly, at least) to more concern regarding the quality of our coworker relationships than do our male counterparts.

Of course, women can be just as competitive as men, but we're often perceived as less likely to voice or act directly on our strong desires to get ahead. We may even deny that we think it's all that important to climb the ladder in the company. After all, many women have been taught to give up their personal needs as part of supporting others. And women are known for "people-pleaser" tendencies that are almost the opposite of the competitive energy cultivated among many men. However, as it becomes increasingly common for women to be appreciated for their career success, rather than just as homemakers or caregivers, I think we will see a shift in female energy in the workplace.

Women also seem more likely to get caught up in the emotional climate of the workplace and less able to stay centered on tasks at hand, especially if someone is upset around them. Also, there can be rifts between single women and those who are married and/or with children. Women with families are often treated with greater flexibility than their single counterparts—often quite unintentionally, but not without impact. I've had many single women report resentment, envy, or jealousy toward women with children whom they perceive to be granted favors or extra flexibility. Many of these single women indicate that they're asked to work longer hours—that their personal time is considered less important.

On the flip side, I've also heard many married women, especially those with children, express that they feel as if they aren't taken seriously as committed professionals. Some report they don't get the best assignments because their bosses may perceive them as less devoted to their jobs.

Again, keep in mind these are simply some trends I've noticed over the years. They may or may not fit for you. Do you notice any different dynamics among female coworkers than among males?

## Women with Men

More and more professions include relatively equal numbers of men and women. Today it's far more the exception than the rule to encounter only other workers of your own gender in the workplace. But while we've advanced in terms of opportunities, many men and women still have no idea how to relate to one another as colleagues rather than as potential mates or friends.

Though the presence of males and females in the same work environment is far more the norm than the exception, it's still relatively new emotional territory for many of us. If you're young and relatively new to the working world, it can be an adjustment to begin dealing with the other gender as fellow professionals. If you've worked in an industry that's traditionally dominated by your gender, you might be subjected to feelings of resentment from members of the opposite gender. Or you might be the one carrying the resentment if your gender has dominated the field and now experiences the other gender as invading its territory. Again, this may not be your experience, but it's something I've heard a lot about from my patients and also personally witnessed in my professional experience.

Both men and women tend to be sensitive to sexism in the workplace. Whether it actually exists in your environment or not, be aware that women often perceive that they are not being treated the same as men. And men often report the experience of reverse sexism—i.e., that they are being looked over while less-qualified women are being advanced. Clearly, sexism doesn't serve either gender well. But we may be likely to misconstrue some things as evidence of what we're looking for, even when it's not really there. I think until sexism is entirely eradicated from our culture, there will be people on the lookout for it. Some won't see it when it's present, and some will see it when it's not. You yourself may not identify with this, but be aware that you're bound to work with some men or women who are prone to misperceptions.

Gender dynamics at work might not be an issue for you. But if anything I've mentioned here has some relevance, then I suggest you give it some thought. To help you bring greater awareness to these issues if they're at all present for you, I recommend you ask yourself the following questions:

1. Do I relate differently to coworkers of my own gender than I do to coworkers of the other?
2. If so, do these different ways of relating serve me well (that is, are they effective in helping me achieve my goals)?
3. Do I hold any stereotypes or prejudices about either gender that get in the way of how I interact in the workplace?

If you discover through your answers that you do struggle with gender issues, don't despair. Just be willing to explore them and change your behavior accordingly.

## Racism and Ageism

As a final note—though one that is no less important—we must all be sensitive to the fact that despite the great deal of progress made in embracing cultural, racial, and age differences among people, we still collectively have a long way to go to overcome deeply ingrained prejudices. And even though most companies have policies that strictly prohibit discrimination, these policies don't necessarily change the way people think. For our society to evolve fully into one that offers equality for all, we need to have an open and loving mindset when it comes to our differences. We shouldn't condone or tolerate bad behavior from anyone, but we certainly don't want to make unfair judgments about others based on skin color, nationality, or age. Anyone who has been a victim of oppression knows how wrong and damaging such behavior can be.

Let's all vow to be conscientious of our own contributions to these ills. Everyone has certain prejudices—you shouldn't feel ashamed for having them. But the way to handle these is to become aware of them and not let them affect our behavior. And by opening up our hearts and minds to respecting differences, we will grow, prosper, and thrive!

▶ *Twelve*

STEP EIGHT—
# Enjoy the Emotional Fruits of Your Labor

By the time you've reached this point of the book, you've gathered a toolbox full of methods for eliminating workplace drama and creating more positive relationships with your boss and coworkers. You've learned to identify the ways you contribute to the mess, and you have new ideas for how to tidy up as much as possible. Ideally, you should feel more confident in your ability to prevent yourself from getting sucked into future drama. But if you're not quite all the way there yet, don't worry. With continued practice and self-discovery, you'll soon be able to improve your skills. Before you know it, spotting the drama traps will become second nature to you.

Granted, life will always be filled with new challenges to conquer. Who knows where your career path will take you over the years? Most likely you'll continue to meet all kinds of new people, each with their own unique dynamics. Some of them will be easier to take than others. But some may push buttons you didn't even know you had. Hence, you must make a commitment to an ongoing process of staying aware of your own behavior and your own styles of interacting. The more you practice these methods, the more you will be able to relax and trust in your progress, but you'll still need to stay alert if you want to ensure continued success.

To help consolidate what you've learned, let's recap the main points. Though they won't help you in all situations, they should certainly offer you a general framework for a more fulfilling workplace experience. Some of these you may have already been doing, but it never hurts to underline them again.

1. Most often, you have a part—however small—in keeping alive the drama in your workplace. Hence, you also have the ability to reduce its magnitude, taking responsibility for the part you do play.
2. Old bruises, especially those originating from childhood, will wreak havoc in your life until you're conscious of how they affect you and you begin to heal them through good self-care, nurturance, and love.
3. The workplace is not the environment in which you should seek this healing. Rather, you should seek repair through support networks, family, friends, loved ones, or professionals.
4. We have the best chance of enriching our workplace experience by taking charge of those things that are in our power to control—that is, our own feelings, behavior, and thoughts. Nothing more, nothing less. At bottom—always keep in mind that it's impossible to change what others do.
5. The more you claim ownership of your choices, the more empowered you become, and the more fulfilling your life will be.

Now, it's time to fully appreciate the hard work you've done thus far. Hey, you got through this book, didn't you? So get out your party hats and noisemakers, it's time to celebrate.

## Celebrating Your Success

Whether you feel like what you've learned is enough to satisfy you for now, or whether you feel that this is just a sample of the work you need to do to improve your workplace relationships, it's critical that you stop and celebrate your accomplishments along the way. And no, I don't mean celebrating with external rewards like buying a new outfit, drinking champagne, or eating the box of chocolates you've been coveting for the last couple of weeks. Though there's certainly nothing wrong with these indulgences, I think you need to offer yourself something more emotionally rewarding, such as acknowledgment and praise for your efforts. You know—all of those strokes that so many of us never got enough of along the way. So carve out a chunk of time to highlight the efforts and progress you've made thus far.

▶ *Praise Exercise*

To make this more meaningful, try the following exercise:

1. Make a list of five of the most important things you've learned concerning how your childhood has affected your experiences in the workplace. Feel free to go back and reread some of the examples of other people's stories to refresh your memory.

2. List five ways that you can improve your workplace experience, being as specific as you can about your unique situation. Try to identify actual behaviors, rather than concepts, so that you can put them into action right away. Below is an example of things that might go on this list.

   - "I will walk away from watercooler gossip without putting in my two cents."
   - "I will assert my right to say 'no,' 'yes,' or 'maybe' as the situation warrants."
   - "I will take a lunch break at least three times per week, regardless of how busy I am."
   - "I will refrain from eavesdropping on coworkers' conversations and focus on my own work instead."
   - "I will not blame others for my choices if I decide to take on more than my share of the workload."

Take your list to work and read it daily. Keep it within eyeshot, or in a drawer or somewhere else handy where you can refer to it often. I'm personally a Post-it junkie. I constantly write myself little reminders of my immediate goals and put them all over the place. Pick a method that works for you.

3. List as many examples as you can of situations where you might have overreacted and made a bigger deal about something than was appropriate. Be compassionate toward yourself and understanding of how your buttons got pushed, and then lovingly make fun of yourself. Tease yourself a bit, and have a good laugh.

4. Write down five goals concerning your workplace relationships that you aim to achieve in the next three months. Make sure these are accomplishable entirely through your own efforts and not dependent on anyone else's cooperation.

Review your lists frequently and modify them as you see fit. Friendly reminders of our mission help to keep us inspired. Whatever you do to highlight your gains thus far, don't skimp on acknowledging and appreciating your energy. It can be very tedious, and often quite grueling, to stay so focused on self-discovery. But I hope and trust you'll find the payoffs worth all of your hard work.

## Seeking Additional Help

This book would not be complete if I didn't include at least a bit about additional help. One of the greatest gifts we can give ourselves is to seek help when we need it. Too often the people who come to me for therapy have waited until matters have gotten really out of hand. By the time these folks enter my office, they feel trapped in a large, covered black hole with no way out. Then, of course, it's much harder to dig oneself back up to the light. It's possible, but far more difficult.

There's clearly nothing wrong with handling things on your own. But why not get a boost from someone else if it's available?

After all, there are so many options for assistance. And to really thrive, you need to learn to use all resources available.

Just as you've done by reading this book, I highly recommend that you continue to use self-help books and articles as resources. If you've been doing the exercises throughout this book, you've most likely identified the various issues that require your attention. Some you might have already been alerted to; others you may have just discovered. By going to the bookstore or surfing the internet, you can search for books specific to the subjects for which you would like more in-depth information. Or you might search for a seminar or wellness workshop in your area. For instance, you might need more information on conquering procrastination or getting rid of shame. This book may have gotten you started, but you might still need more.

In addition, there may be an abundance of resources available to you through your workplace. Many companies have a human resources department that has a specific mandate to help employees with issues concerning both work-related and personal-related matters. If your company has an EAP (Employee Assistance Program), you might be able to receive a counseling session (or several counseling sessions) free of charge. Find out what's available to you, and take advantage of these resources.

Of course, sometimes we want to ensure our privacy, or we feel our issues are such that we need to have an ongoing therapeutic relationship with someone completely separate from our workplace. Though resources for help in the workplace *should* remain protected and confidential, clearly there's a bigger chance of someone getting wind of your seeking help. If this is the case, you should consider seeking outside counseling.

Though I would love to believe that everyone has a positive attitude about psychotherapy, I would be naïve if I really thought this was the norm. We as a society still have a great deal of confusion and prejudice concerning people who seek therapy. I should hope that you personally don't hold any negative stigmas about seeking psychotherapy with a qualified professional, but just in case you do, let me offer a few words of reassurance. There's nothing to be ashamed of if you need or desire professional guidance. There's nothing "wrong" with you. Psychotherapy is about promoting health and well-being, not about being damaged or defective and needing to be fixed. Seeking help is not a sign of weakness. Quite the contrary. Seeking help is a sign of strength.

Also, looking into childhood experiences to help draw connections to problems in the workplace may not be sufficient for you. If you're continually struggling, you could be suffering from any number of conditions that affect your basic functioning—like depression, anxiety, posttraumatic stress disorder, or attention deficit disorder, to name a few. If so, then you will need a professional evaluation to learn about all options for treatment. Hey, if you had heart palpitations and trouble breathing, I'd like to believe that you'd go get a physical exam. So, if you're suffering emotional distress and the changes you're trying to make don't seem to be working, why not seek a psychological evaluation? Our emotional and psychological well-being should be considered just as important as our physical health.

If finances are of concern, check out your health insurance benefits. Unfortunately, psychotherapy isn't covered by every health plan, but many companies are starting to grasp the importance of the mind-body connection, and as a result, they're opting to offer mental-health benefits. Whatever the case, don't hesitate to call your health insurance carrier and find out what is and isn't covered.

If your health insurance carrier doesn't provide mental-health coverage, try checking out lower-cost clinics. Contacting your local hospital or county psychological society can help get you started on your search. Don't hold back for too long. If your own efforts fail to yield the results you're seeking, then the sooner you seek out further assistance, the sooner you'll be reaping the benefits.

Should you opt to pursue counseling, make sure to seek out someone who would be a good fit and who will serve your needs. I recommend that you seek a licensed practitioner who has specific experience with the issues you face. If the cost is prohibitive, you can seek out a registered intern or psychological assistant who receives ongoing supervision from a licensed psychotherapist. People who hold a master's, PhD, or MD degrees in the fields of psychology, social work, or psychiatry all may be qualified to practice psychotherapy as long as they've been properly trained and licensed in their state. Make sure to find someone with these qualifications before selecting a therapist.

Keep in mind that this selection process should be taken very seriously. Though you certainly can use the telephone directory, I recommend getting a referral from a trusted source (e.g., friend, relative, community-service organization). If you're going to share the intimate details of your life with someone, you need to be very careful about picking someone who can offer you helpful guidance.

More recently, there is a new breed of helpers on the scene known as "life coaches." Increasingly, life coaches are sought out to help people with both life and work issues, almost as an alternative to counseling or therapy. While I certainly believe that many of these coaches offer extremely valuable help, as of now, there is no regulatory body that governs the ethics and practice of coaching. Pretty much anyone can call herself a coach and charge whatever the client will pay. So choose wisely if you go in this direction. And please understand that coaching is different from psychotherapy!

Whatever steps you choose in order to continue on your journey, please remember these two things. One, be patient. And, two, be self-loving. If the only thing you take away from this book is a greater appreciation for your need for nurturance and compassion, then you've gained a lot.

Please feel free to go back through the pages and revisit the chapters most meaningful to you. I've had lots of people share with me that something they've read or heard didn't register right away. Months from now, or maybe even years, once you've gained new experiences and new wisdom, you might find a pearl that's always been on your path. Cherish all of your moments of insight, and let all of your experiences inspire you.

Now give yourself a big hug and go get 'em, tiger!

## ACKNOWLEDGEMENTS

I am very grateful to have been able to write this book and have it published. I hope it will reach as many of the millions of people as possible who desire to overcome drama in the workplace. Though I would have written the book regardless of whether others backed me or not, I was truly blessed to have received an abundance of encouragement and support from all of those within my inner circle. To anyone important in my life whom I've not specifically addressed, please know that you're contributions have not gone unnoticed!

To Linda Konner, my agent, for your never-wavering comfort, assistance, and reassurance. You've helped me refine my ideas and strive for the best, even through my moments of resistance. Your continual fortitude and optimism (and of course, a few much needed grammar-checks) kept me determined, even when I doubted my own path. Having you in my corner has been a true gift to cherish!

To Doug Seibold, my editor and publisher. Thank you ever so much for seeing the value in this book and for giving it your all to make it come to life. Your dedication and vision of success could not be matched by any other. I could not have asked for a better guy to be the backbone for this project. You've given me the best publishing experience any author could ever hope for!

To all of my friends whom I couldn't begin to list without fearing that I would miss someone important. I hope you know who you are. And I treasure each and every one of you. Thank you for listening to me babble on and on about all the trials and tribulations of being an author and for standing by me, even though I have not been the best of friends throughout the writing process. I am very fortunate to be the recipient of so much love. And special thanks to Ruth for generously giving your precious time and energy to read through the manuscript as it was a work in progress and for contributing invaluable feedback from your professional background in Human Resources.

To all of the bosses and coworkers with whom I've acted out my own drama. My relationships with all of you have been tremendously inspirational when it came to the writing of this book. And to all of my clients who have been willing to share their stories of vulnerability, and to entrust me with their care. Were it not for your unsparing accounts of the challenges in your lives and your positive transformations, there would be no book.

To Tiffany, my dear daughter. Through your unconditional acceptance, support, and belief in me, I've truly learned the importance of balance and of the preciousness of life and love. Being your mother gives me the greatest joy one could ever imagine and makes me so proud. You are a gem!

To Rachel, Remi, and Delainey, the other extremely important children in my life. Thank you ever so much for your gifts of love. And special thanks to my sister, Cheryl; my father, Al; and my stepmother, Dora—for always making the time to share in my excitement and for cheering me on in all my endeavors.

Last but certainly not least, thanks to Chris, my best friend, intimate partner, and all-around great guy. It never ceases to amaze me how much you trust in my abilities, support my goals, and hold me in such high esteem. I don't always understand what you see, but I sure am glad you are in my life. Your strength has carried us through many storms and I will forever be grateful for the passion that keeps us together.

With love and my deepest appreciation to all of you!

## ABOUT THE AUTHOR

Debra Mandel, PhD, is a clinical psychologist, speaker, columnist, and media expert with more than twenty years of experience dealing with relationships, depression, anxiety, survivors of abuse, and general life concerns. She regularly appears on national television and radio, sharing her expertise on a variety of topics. Some of her many TV appearances include the shows *Starting Over, The 750 Pound Man, Thirty Days* with Morgan Spurlock, *My Big Fat Obnoxious Fiance,* and several others yet to be aired. She was also featured as a regular guest expert on the syndicated TV talk show, *The Larry Elder Show,* and hosted her own radio show, "Shrink Rap," which aired weekly on KCSN in Los Angeles. She is the author of the book *Healing the Sensitive Heart* (Adams Media, 2003 and Airleaf Publishing, 2005) and two CDs, *Creating Healthy Boundaries in the Workplace* and *The Abuser Friendly Syndrome.* You can contact Dr. Debra on the web at www.drdebraonline.com for more information.